Crossroads Café
WORKTEXT B

The publication of *Crossroads Café* was directed by the members of the Heinle & Heinle Secondary and Adult ESL Publishing Team.

Editorial Director:	Roseanne Mendoza
Senior Production Services Coordinator:	Lisa McLaughlin
Market Development Director:	Andy Martin

Also participating in the publication of the program were:

Vice President and Publisher, ESL:	Stanley Galek
Developmental Editor:	Nancy Mann Jordan
Senior Assistant Editor:	Sally Conover
Production Editor:	Maryellen Killeen
Manufacturing Coordinator:	Mary Beth Hennebury
Director of Global ELT Training and Development:	Evelyn Nelson
Full Service Design and Production:	PC&F, Inc.

Manufactured in the United States of America.

ISBN: 0-8384-66060

Heinle & Heinle is a division of International Thomson Publishing, Inc.

Photo Credits
Episodes 1, 2, 3, 4, 5, 6, 9, 10, 13, 14, 16, 17, 18: Stanley Newton
Episodes 7, 8, 11, 12, 15, 19, 20, 21, 22, 23, 24, 25, 26: Jane O'Neal
Episode 15, pages 33 and 34: K. Lynn Savage

Crossroads Café

WORKTEXT B

K. Lynn Savage • Patricia Mooney Gonzalez • Mary McMullin
with Kathleen Santopietro Weddel

HEINLE & HEINLE PUBLISHERS

I(T)P *An International Thomson Publishing Company*

Boston, Massachusetts 02116 U.S.A.

*New York • London • Bonn • Boston • Detroit • Madrid • Melbourne • Mexico City • Paris •
Singapore • Tokyo • Toronto • Washington • Albany, NY • Belmont, CA • Cincinnati, OH*

Table of Contents and

	Title	Ways to Learn	Function/Structure*
14	**Life Goes On**	Make a List	Describing Things: *bad; very bad; too bad to eat*
15	**Breaking Away**	Make Inferences	Talking about Likes and Dislikes: *like . . .; like to . . .*
16	**The Bottom Line**	Try and Try Again	Reporting Information: *told me to . . .; told me about . . .; says . . .; said . . .*
17	**United We Stand**	Read for Meaning	Making Complaints: *doesn't work; is leaking*
18	**Opportunity Knocks**	Be Open to Learning	Comparing Things: *more tired than . . .; better than . . .*
19	**The People's Choice**	Take a Risk	Making Promises: *promise that . . .; promise to . . .*
20	**Outside Looking In**	Take Notes	Giving Advice: *should . . .; had better . . .*
21	**Walls and Bridges**	Teach Others	Asking For and Offering Help: *Please fix it for me; Would you fix it for me?; I'd be glad to fix it for you.*
22	**Helping Hands**	Practice Often	Asking For and Giving Permission: *May; Can; Would you mind if . . .*
23	**The Gift**	Know Your Learning Style	Making Invitations: *I'd like you to . . .; How about . . .*
24	**All's Well That Ends Well**	Look for Humor	Talking about the Future: *will . . .; going to . . .*
25	**Comings and Goings**	Compliment Yourself	Talking about Future Plans and Possibilities: *going to . . .; might . . .*
26	**Winds of Change**	Evaluate Your Learning	Talking about Necessity: *have to . . .; must . . .*

*Crossroads Café is correlated to The New Grammar In Action series 1–3.
Please order The Heinle Grammar Correlation Booklet, ISBN 0-8384-9895-7.

Scope and Sequence

SCANS* AT-A-GLAN

Video Time (min: sec) Worktext	Crossroads Café Lesson Plans	SCANS Discussion Focus
14 Life Goes On		
• 1:22–2:49 • 5:30–7:56 Text p. 13 • Text p. 12	• Managing the café during Mr. Brashov's hospitalization • Culture Clip: Hospitals • What Do You Think?	• Interpersonal: *teamwork* • Systems: *understand organizational systems* • Information: *interpret*
15 Breaking Away		
• 3:55–6:28 21:23–24:14 • 8:17–12:13 Text p. 27 • Text p. 26	• Preparing for rejection Henry's parents and his girl friend's parents meet. • Culture Clip: Intercultural Relationships • What Do You Think?	• Personal: *self esteem* • Thinking: *solve problems* • Sociability: *understanding adaptability* • Interpersonal: *persuade*
16 The Bottom Line		
• 4:22–5:21 • 12:55–14:17 • 15:29–17:12 • Text p. 40	• Mr. Brashov tries to apply for a loan • The banker visits the restaurant. • Word Play: Reporting Information • What Do You Think?	• Systems: *monitor and correct performance* • Thinking: *recognize problem, create a plan of action* • Basic Skills: *organize and communicate ideas* • Thinking: *solve problems*
17 United We Stand		
• 15:22–15:59 • 6:16–8:40 Text p. 55 • Text p. 54	• Rosa organizes a tenants' meeting. • Culture Clip: Tenant and Landlord Responsibilities • What Do You Think?	• Thinking: *recognize problems, devise action plan* • Systems: *work within the system* • Systems: *organizational systems*
18 Opportunity Knocks		
• 4:57–7:54 • 17:51–20:21 Text p. 69 • Text p. 68	• Jamal is offered a job. • Culture Clip: Worker Safety • What Do You Think?	• Personal: *choose ethical courses of action* • Systems: *understand and operate effectively* • Personal: *integrity*
19 The People's Choice		
• 3:15–5:54 • 9:44–12:10 Text p. 83 • Text p. 82	• Jess runs for City Council. • Culture Clip: Local Government • What Do You Think?	• Personal: *self-worth* • Systems: *understand organizational systems* • Information: *evaluate*

***SCANS** is an acronym for the Secretary's Commission on Achieving Necessary Skills (U.S. Department of Labor, 1991)

CE LESSON PLANS

Video Time (min: sec) Worktext	Crossroads Café Lesson Plans	SCANS Discussion Focus
20 Outside Looking In		
• 24:38–25:39 • 16:28–19:30 Text p. 97 • Text p. 96	• Rosa translates at a business party • Culture Clip: Raising Children • What Do You Think?	• Basic Skills: *speaking—communicates orally* • Interpersonal: *cultural diversity* • Personal: *self worth*
21 Walls and Bridges		
• 12:19–14:22 • 22:48–25:31 • 18:55–22:16 Text p. 111 • Text p. 110	• Rosa and Chris go to Mr. Hernandez's tailor shop. • Talking about daughters. • Culture Clip: Becoming a Citizen • What Do You Think?	• Interpersonal: *negotiate* • Interpersonal Skills: *teach others new skills* • Systems: *understand organizational system* • Thinking: *solve problems*
22 Helping Hands		
• 21:21–24:11 • 7:10–9:57 Text p. 125 • Text p. 124	• Helping Frank get a job • Culture Clip: Financial Difficulties • What Do You Think?	• Thinking: *think creatively* • Resources: *allocate money to meet objectives* • Information: *interpret and communicate*
23 The Gift		
• 22:58–25:06 • 10:48–12:47 Text p. 139 • Text p. 138	• Planning Mr. Brashov's surprise birthday party • Culture Clip: Taxes • What Do You Think?	• Thinking: *think creatively* and *make decisions* • Systems: *understand social systems* • Information: *analyze and communicate*
24 All's Well That Ends Well		
• 8:01–10:20 Text p. 153 • Text p. 152	• Culture Clip: Wedding Customs • What Do You Think?	• Interpersonal: *cultural diversity* • Interpersonal: *communicate ideas to justify position*
25 Comings and Goings		
• 8:26–9:57 • 9:59–11:48 Text p. 167 • Text p. 166	• Jamal receives job offer • Culture Clip: Returning to Your Home Culture • What Do You Think?	• Personal: *assess self, set goals* • Thinking: *solve problems* • Interpersonal: *persuade*
26 Winds of Change		
• 11:43–15:18 Text p. 181 • Text p. 180	• Culture Clip: Achieving Goals • What Do You Think?	• Personal: *set personal goals* • Personal: *set personal goals*

Acknowledgments

Rigorous review by members of the National Academic Council contributed to the initial design as well as the philosophical underpinnings of the products: Fiona Armstrong, Office of Adult and Continuing Education, New York City Board of Education; Janet Buongiorno, Adult Literacy Enhancement Center, Edison, New Jersey; Yvonne Cadiz, Adult and Community Education Program, Hillsborough County Public Schools, Florida; the late Jim Dodd, Bureau of Adult and Community Education, Department of Education, Florida; Chela Gonzalez, Metropolitan Adult Education Program, San Jose, California; Chip Harman, United States Information Agency, Washington, D.C.; Edwina Hoffman, Dade County Public Schools, Florida; Maggie Steinz, Illinois State Board of Education; Dennis Terdy, Adult Learning Resource Center, Des Plaines, Illinois; Inaam Mansour, Arlington Education and Employment Program, Arlington, Virginia; Fortune Valenty, Perth Amboy Public Schools, New Jersey; Kathleen Santopietro Weddel, Colorado Department of Education.

Collaboration among the Institute for Social Research at the University of Michigan, Interwest Applied Research in Portland, Oregon, and the National Center for Adult Literacy provided evaluation data that guided modification of student materials and development of teacher/tutor materials. Guiding and directing the evaluations were Jere Johnston, Dan Wagner, Regie Stites, and Evelyn Brzezinski. Participating pilot sites included the following: Alhambra School District, California; The Brooklyn Adult Learning Center, New York City Board of Education; Dade County Public Schools, Florida; Mt. Hood Community College, Portland, Oregon; Jewish Family Services, San Diego, California; Polish Welfare Association, Chicago, Illinois; One-Stop Immigration Center, Los Angeles, California; Even Start Program, Northside Independent School District, San Antonio, Texas; Margarita R. Huantes, Learning and Leadership Development Center, San Antonio, Texas; San Diego Community College District.

The collaboration with INTELECOM resulted in provocative stories, which provided meaningful contexts for the *Worktext's* activities. Thank you to Sarah for graciously providing whatever was needed and holding everything together during the most frenetic stages of the project; Peter and Glenn for providing entertaining and relevant story lines; Bob for keeping everyone properly focused; and Sally, for her leadership as well as her commitment and involvement in all aspects of the project.

Extensive experience of Heinle & Heinle and its staff in publishing language-learning materials ensured quality print materials. The authors wish to thank Nancy Mann, *Worktexts* editor, for her professionalism and expertise; Sally Conover, *Photo Stories* editor, for the dedication, patience, and attention to detail that the Photo Stories required; Lisa McLaughlin, production coordinator, for ensuring that the extremely tight production schedule was met without sacrificing quality; Maryellen Killeen, production editor, for her infinite patience and good humor in sorting through the hundreds of photos for the Photo Stories; Roseanne Mendoza, acquisitions editor, for her willingness to take the risks that the development of cutting edge products requires and for her commitment to fighting for the things she believes in.

Lynn would like to thank Roseanne at Heinle & Heinle for inviting her to participate in the project and for the good times working and growing together again; Jann for the fun times in the initial development and the from-the-heart comments in her ongoing review; Sally at INTELECOM for her accessibility day and night; and sister Gail, who listens well.

Pat would like to thank Roseanne at Heinle & Heinle for including her in this meaningful project and for her support during challenging times; Lynn for being a good listener, for patient assistance in seeing the "big picture" and for providing pep talks as needed; Sally and Nancy at Heinle & Heinle for their guidance and insightful comments, no matter how crazy the production schedule. Pat would also like to thank "Berry" and Diane for their support, understanding, and technical assistance throughout the duration of this project.

Mary would like to thank Kirk, Mom, Dad, Helen, Toula, and the rest of the family for keeping her focused on the important things. She is also grateful to Lilly and Tommy for the funny things they do.

To the Learner: About *Crossroads Café*

These pages explain what the *Crossroads Café* program is and how to use it. If you have problems understanding these explanations, ask someone to read and discuss them with you. If you start with a clear idea of how to use *Crossroads Café* correctly, your chances for success will be great.

Crossroads Café provides a unique method to learn English. The use of a television series and videos will help you improve your English. The *Crossroads Café* books are excellent tools for helping you use the television series or the videos to improve your listening, speaking, reading, and writing in English. The next section explains how each piece of the program can help you. It also answers some important questions about the series and how it should be used.

What Is *Crossroads Café*?

Crossroads Café is a course for studying English. The course teaches English as it entertains. It also helps you understand North American culture and use that understanding to live and work in the culture more successfully.

What Are the Parts of the Program?

There are three parts of the program for learners.
- The 26 television programs or the videos
- The two *Photo Stories* books
- The two *Worktexts*

You will use television programs or videos with the *Photo Stories,* the *Worktexts,* or both to learn English.

What Are the Television Programs?

The television programs are the most important part of the *Crossroads Café* program. There are 26 thirty-minute episodes that tell the story of a group of hard-working, determined people whose lives come together at a small neighborhood restaurant called Crossroads Café. Some of them are newcomers to the United States. Others have families that have been here for one or many generations. These people slowly create a successful neighborhood restaurant. During the 26 episodes, *Crossroads Café* tells of the successes and the failures, the joys and the sadness, and especially the learning experiences of the owner of the café, the people who work in it, their families, friends, acquaintances, neighbors, and the people they must cooperate with to be successful in their work and in their lives. The story is sometimes funny, sometimes sad, but always entertaining. The large picture above shows the six main characters in *Crossroads Café*. The smaller pictures around it show the characters in their lives outside the café.

These are the people you will learn about in *Crossroads Café.* You will be able to understand many of the problems they face and share many of their feelings. You will learn from their experiences—learn English and learn something about North American culture. You will also discover new ways to learn—which can be new paths to success for you in an English-speaking culture.

Most of each thirty-minute program deals with the story of the café and its six characters. But there are two other pieces in each episode that are especially good for people who want to learn English and understand North American culture. In every episode, there is a short section called "Word Play." "Word Play" always shows and explains some special way English is used in that episode. It combines cartoons, illustrations, and scenes from the episode to teach how to use English for a special purpose. For example, "Word Play" presents ways to ask for help, make suggestions, or, as this picture shows, make complaints.

The second special section that is part of every episode is the "Culture Clip." It helps you understand North American culture. You can agree or disagree with the behavior the "Culture Clip" shows, but this section will always help you think about your ideas on culture, in your own country and in your life today. This can help you understand and deal with cultural differences.

How Do I Use the Television Programs or Videos?

You can use the program if you are any of these types of learner. Here's how each type can best use the television programs or the videos.

1. **The Independent Learner.** You want to study the language on your own— possibly with the help of a tutor, a friend, a neighbor, or a family member. You may have seen an episode of *Crossroads Café* on television, or you may have heard about it from someone else—a friend or a family member. You may have seen ads for the program in a store or a library. You ordered the *Crossroads Café* program on your own because you wanted to learn English at home, by yourself or with someone else.

2. **The Distant Learner.** You study in a distance-learning program in a school. You may talk to or see your teacher once a week, once every two weeks, or once a month. But most of your study will be done alone, using the *Crossroads Café* materials. Your teacher may tell you to watch *Crossroads Café* one or more times each week and do the activities in the *Worktexts,* the *Photo Stories,* or both. When you meet with your teacher—and perhaps with other students too—you will talk about what you saw and learned. You may also do some activities from the *Teacher's Resource Book* with the other students and your teacher.

3. The Classroom Learner. You study in a regular class with a teacher in a school. You will use the *Crossroads Café* books—*Worktexts, Photo Stories,* or both—in your class. Your teacher will ask you to watch *Crossroads Café* programs and do some of the activities in your book at home. In class, you will work with other students to do more activities in the *Worktext* or the *Photo Stories* and other activities from the *Teacher's Resource Book.* Your teacher may also show important pieces of the episodes again in class and discuss them with the students.

How Do I Use the *Worktexts?*

Each of the two *Crossroads Café Worktexts* contains thirteen episodes—half the episodes in the complete series. Every *Worktext* lesson has the same parts, which you will use to practice and improve your English before and after you watch the television or video.

The *Worktexts* are carefully written to help learners at three different levels of English study—high beginning, low intermediate, and high intermediate. You can "grow" with the program by using the same *Worktexts* and videos over and over as you acquire more English. Here's how these multi-level *Worktexts* can work for you.

The different activities in each section of the books are marked with colored stars— one, two, or three stars for the three different levels of learners. Here are two possible ways to use the *Worktexts.*

1. If you are working alone, without a teacher, try to work through all three levels in the first unit to see which level suits you best. Be honest with yourself. If you check your answers and see that you've made mistakes at a certain level, it's best to choose the level below that one. If you have a teacher or a tutor, he or she will probably choose a level for you. After you know your level, always do the activities for that level, as well as the activities for the levels before it. For example, let's say you decide you are a two-star learner. In every section, you will do the one-star activity first and then the two-star activity. If you are a three-star learner, you will do the one-star and the two-star activities before you do the three-star activity. Don't skip the lower-level activities. They are the warm-up practice that can help you succeed when you reach your own level.

2. In each section, go as far as you can in the star system. For example, in the first activity in an episode, you may be able to do both the one-star and the two-star activities easily. However, you may not be able to complete the three-star activity. So, stop after the two-star activity and move on to the next section. In the second section, you may be able to all three levels of stars easily, or you may only be able to do the one-star activity. Always begin with the one-star activity and, if you succeed, then move on to the more advanced activities. If you have problems with an activity, get help right away from your teacher or tutor, or from someone whose English is better than yours.

Remember, if you are studying alone you can choose one of those two ways of working. If you have a teacher or a tutor, that person can help you decide how to work. But if you have problems with any activity, always try to get help immediately from your teacher, your tutor, or someone else who knows more English than you. That way, you can understand what to do and how to correct yourself.

How Can the *Worktext* Activities Help Me Learn?

The *Worktext* activities do three things:

1. They help you understand the story on the video.

2. They provide language practice.

3. They ask you to think about, talk about, and write about your ideas.

Understanding the Story: To help you understand the story, the *Worktext* has activities for you to do before and after you watch the episode.

Before you watch, you can do three things:

- Look at the big picture on the first page for the episode. Look at the title. Then try to guess what the story is about. Talk about your ideas with someone.

- Then look at the six pictures in the "Before You Watch" section. Talk about the pictures with someone. Do the exercises that go with the pictures. Check your answers by looking at the answer key in the back of the book.

- Finally, read the questions in the "Focus for Watching" section. If you do not understand some words, use your dictionary, or ask someone what the words mean.

After you watch the episode, turn to the "After You Watch" activities in your *Worktext*. In these activities, you will do two things:

- You will match key people from the story with the focus questions.

- You will answer questions about important parts of the story and then you will put those parts in order.

Practicing the Language helps you develop your English language skills. This section of the *Worktext* gives you special activities to do after you watch the television or video. These next three sections will help you improve your grammar, your reading, and your writing.

Your New Language presents grammar for a special purpose. For example, you will learn to use commands to tell someone to do something. Or you will learn to use *can* and *know how to* to talk about what you are able to do. Here is a good way to do these activities:

- Watch "Word Play" on the video again, if possible.

- Complete the "Your New Language" section of your *Worktext*.

- Check your answers. Use the "Answer Key" in the back of the *Worktexts*.

- Practice the conversations in "Your New Language" with someone.

In Your Community presents the kind of reading you find in your everyday life. Here is a good way to do these activities:

- Answer the questions about the reading.
- Check your answers. Use the "Answer Key" in the back of your *Worktext*.
- Look for the same kind of reading in the town or city where you live.
- Compare the reading you find with the one in the *Worktext*.

Read and Write presents something that a person in *Crossroads Café* wrote. It may be a letter, a note, a diary page, or a newspaper article. Here is a good way to do these activities:

- Answer the questions about the main ideas of the writing.
- Guess the meaning of the words in the vocabulary exercises.
- Use your experiences to write about something similar.
- Share your writing with someone.

Two sections of each *Worktext* unit have exercises that ask you to give your opinions about something that happened in the story. These sections are called "What Do You Think?" and "Culture Clip."

Here is a good way to work through the **What Do You Think?** activities:

- Think about things people in the story have done or opinions they have expressed.
- Share your ideas with someone.

Here is a good way to work through the **Culture Clip** activities:

- Watch the "Culture Clip" on the video again, if possible.
- Identify the main ideas from the "Culture Clip."
- Give your own opinion about a situation related to the "Culture Clip."

Check Your English is the last activity in each unit. It is a review of vocabulary, grammar, and reading. You can check your answers with the "Answer Key" in the back of your *Worktext*.

What Are the *Photo Stories?*

The *Crossroads Café Photo Stories* do these things:

- They help you understand the story before you watch the video.
- They ask you questions to help you understand parts of the story.
- They help you improve your vocabulary.
- They help you review after you watch.

The *Photo Stories* can help you if you know a little English or a lot of English:

- They can be special books for beginning learners of English. Learners study the pictures from the video. These pictures have the words from the story in them. This combination of words and photos makes learning English easy. If you speak Spanish, you may have read *fotonovelas*, or *telefotonovelas*. The *Photo Stories* look very much like those books, and they tell interesting stories, too.

- They are also for more advanced students of English. They can be an extra help for you if you are using the *Worktexts*. You can use the *Photo Story* to preview each television or video episode. First read the *Photo Story* and then do the exercises. Then, when you watch the episode, you will be prepared to understand what is happening and know what the characters will say.

This sample page shows how the *Photo Stories* tell the story of the video and help you read to find the meaning.

This sample page shows one type of activity you will do after you read the story.

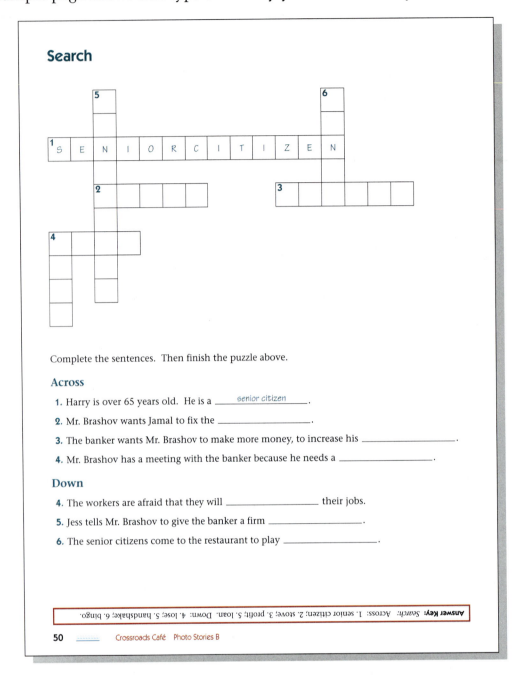

Search

Complete the sentences. Then finish the puzzle above.

Across

1. Harry is over 65 years old. He is a _____senior citizen_____.

2. Mr. Brashov wants Jamal to fix the _____.

3. The banker wants Mr. Brashov to make more money, to increase his _____.

4. Mr. Brashov has a meeting with the banker because he needs a _____.

Down

4. The workers are afraid that they will _____ their jobs.

5. Jess tells Mr. Brashov to give the banker a firm _____.

6. The senior citizens come to the restaurant to play _____.

Answer Key: *Search:* Across: 1. senior citizen; 2. stove; 3. profit; 5. loan. Down: 4. lose; 5. handshake; 6. bingo.

Special Questions about *Crossroads Café*

Learners of English and their teachers and tutors sometimes ask these questions about *Crossroads Café*.

What if I can't understand everything in the television or video episodes? Don't worry if you can't understand some language in the episodes. Even if you don't understand a lot of language, you can still learn from watching. You will often be able to guess what is happening in the story. This is because sometimes the people use actions that help you understand the meaning of their words. Also, sometimes they will look happy, surprised, or even angry when they speak. These facial expressions help you guess what they are saying. Learn to watch for these clues. They can help you understand the story. Good language learners know how to use these clues to help themselves. With *Crossroads Café,* you will learn to develop successful language-learning habits.

What if I can't understand the way some of the characters speak? In *Crossroads Café,* several important characters were either born in the U.S. or arrived when they were very young. They speak English without accents:

- Katherine is from the Midwest.
- Jess is from the South.
- Henry was born in China, but immigrated to the U.S. before he started school.

But some characters are from other parts of the world:

- Mr. Brashov is from Eastern Europe.
- Rosa was born in the U.S., but she grew up in Latin America.
- Jamal is from the Middle East.

These characters, like you, are still improving their English pronunciation, although they always use correct grammar. It will help you to hear many different pronunciations of English. In North America, and in the world in general, people speak English in many different ways. In schools, at work, and in the streets, other people need to understand them to communicate successfully with them. Becoming accustomed to hearing speakers from different cultures and different ethnic groups is a skill successful English speakers need to develop in our modern world.

What if the English is too fast for me? In *Crossroads Café,* the characters speak at a natural speed. Their speech is not artificially slow. In the real world, very few people talk slowly to help learners of English, so in *Crossroads Café* you will hear English spoken naturally. This will be helpful to you in the long run. But the *Crossroads Café* course can give you extra help as you become accustomed to hearing English at a normal pace. Here are four ways you can use the program to get this help:

- You can preview and review the story by using the *Photo Stories,* the *Worktext,* or both.
- If you meet with your teacher and your class, your teacher may use the video version to show again some important pieces of the episode you already watched.
- Your teacher may also show some pieces of a video episode *before* you see the complete episode at home on television.
- You can record complete episodes of *Crossroads Café* with a VCR and then play them back for yourself again and again. Or you may want to buy some or all of the video episodes by calling 1-800-ESL-BY-TV (1-800-375-2988) or 1-800-354-9706.

Why should I have a study partner? Learning a language means learning to communicate with others. Using videos and television programs to learn a language has many advantages, but seeing the programs and doing the reading, writing, and thinking activities in the *Worktext* is not enough. Having a study partner gives you the opportunity to practice your new language skills. That person can be another *Crossroads Café* English learner. It can be a wonderful shared experience to do the lessons and watch the videos with a partner who is also learning English. But your partner could also be someone who knows more English than you do. It can be someone who is not studying with the *Crossroads Café* materials—someone like a relative who knows English and can help you—perhaps a son or a daughter, a husband or a wife, or any other family member. Or the partner can be a neighbor, a person who works with you, a friend, or any person who knows more English than you do. And, finally, the partner can be a formal or informal tutor—a librarian, a high-school student, or someone who used to be a teacher. Any of these people can help make the time you spend learning English more productive. If your partner knows more English than you do, he or she can use the *Crossroads Café Partner Guide*. The *Partner Guide* is small and easy to use, but it has excellent ideas for helping learners of English.

Crossroads Café—Summaries of Units 1 to 13

1	Opening Day	Victor Brashov is ready to open a new restaurant, but the restaurant doesn't have a name or workers.
2	Growing Pains	Henry has problems with working at the café. A health and safety inspector visits the café.
3	Worlds Apart	Rosa's boyfriend arrives from Mexico, and she must make a difficult decision. Mr. Brashov has trouble sleeping.
4	Who's the Boss?	Jamal sees two old friends. They think he's the owner of the café.
5	Lost and Found	Katherine's son has behavior problems in school. He gets help from someone. Jess and Carol's house is robbed.
6	Time is Money	An efficiency expert comes to look at the café. Rosa has problems with her night school class.
7	Fish Out of Water	Mr. Brashov's brother arrives from Romania. He finds that life in the United States is different from life in his country.
8	Family Matters	Katherine takes a second job to make more money. Rosa teaches Henry to dance.
9	Rush to Judgment	Jamal is a suspect in a robbery. Henry's grandparents get lost in the city.
10	Let the Buyer Beware	Mr. Brashov meets a woman who promises to improve the café's business. He goes out on several dates with her. Katherine also goes out on a date.
11	No Vacancy	Rosa wants to move into a new apartment, but she has problems. Henry works on a journalism project.
12	Turning Points	Someone breaks into the café. Rosa learns to drive.
13	Trading Places	The café employees change jobs for a day. Jess and Carol have problems at home.

14 Life Goes On

In this unit you will:

- describe things
- read medicine labels
- write a letter
- describe hospital rules

Ways to Learn

In the hospital, Mr. Brashov **makes a list** of things his employees need to do. He makes a list to **organize** the work.

Make a List

Check (✔) the lists you make in English to help you remember.

- ☐ shopping (*groceries, clothing . . .*)
- ☐ errands (*go to bank, go to post office . . .*)
- ☐ plans for the day (*study, clean kitchen . . .*)
- ☐ steps to do a job (*at work, prepare for a party . . .*)
- ☐ new English words
- ☐ things to take on a trip (*tooth brush, soap, comb . . .*)
- ☐ gifts to buy (*holidays, birthdays . . .*)
- ☐ other: _____

On Your Own

Last week I **made a list** of _____.

The list helped me remember . . . Check (✔)

- ☐ vocabulary
- ☐ pronunciation
- ☐ grammar
- ☐ other: _____

Next week I will make a list of _____

to help me remember _____.

Before You Watch

Look at the pictures. What do you see?

1.

2.

3.

4.

5.

6.

✪ What do you see in each picture? Write the number of the picture next to the word.

  <u>3</u> medicine   _____ package

  _____ food tray   _____ darkness

  _____ nurse   _____ counter

✪✪ What is happening? Write the number of the picture next to the sentence.

  <u>5</u> A young woman gives a package to Jess.

  _____ Mr. Brashov is angry at the nurse.

  _____ Jess explains some things to Rosa and Katherine.

  _____ The patient has something to eat.

  _____ There is a problem with the lights.

  _____ Mr. Brashov takes his medicine.

✪✪✪ Write one question you have about each picture. Then read your questions to someone.

1. Who is Rosa talking to? _____

2. _____

3. _____

4. _____

5. _____

6. _____

Focus For Watching   Read the questions. Then watch.

✪ 1. Who goes to the hospital?
   2. Who takes care of the patients?

✪✪ 1. Who does Mr. Brashov's job while he is in the hospital?
    2. Who shares the hospital room with Mr. Brashov?

✪✪✪ 1. Who tells Mr. Brashov he is on a strict diet?
     2. Who comes to the café to leave a gift for Mr. Brashov?

After You Watch

What do you remember? Match each question with the correct picture. You can use a picture more than once.

⭐ 1. Who goes to the hospital?

a. Brenda

2. Who takes care of the patients?

b. Jess

⭐⭐ 1. Who does Mr. Brashov's job while he is in the hospital?

2. Who shares the hospital room with Mr. Brashov?

c. Mr. Brashov

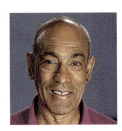

d. Anna Brashov

⭐⭐⭐ 1. Who tells Mr. Brashov he is on a strict diet?

2. Who comes to the café to leave a gift for Mr. Brashov?

e. Mr. Joe Jenkins

⭐ Read the sentences. Circle Yes or No.

1. Mr. Brashov has stomach problems. YES (NO)
2. Brenda takes care of the patients in the hospital. YES NO
3. Katherine takes charge of the café while Mr. Brashov is in the hospital. YES NO
4. Mr. Brashov finds out he has a grandson. YES NO

✪✪ Put the sentences in order. Number 1 to 4.

_____ While in the hospital, Mr. Brashov meets Joe Jenkins.

_____ After a few days in the hospital, Mr. Brashov goes home.

_____ He is happy because he receives a gift from his daughter.

__1__ Mr. Brashov is in the hospital because he had a heart attack.

✪✪✪ Write the story. Use the four sentences above. Add these three sentences.
Then close the book and tell the story to someone.

• When Mr. Brashov returns to Crossroads Café, he says he feels glad to be back.
• Joe Jenkins likes to talk and joke with the nurse.
• Mr. Brashov feels sad when Mr. Jenkins dies.

Mr. Brashov is in the hospital because he had a heart attack. While in the hospital,
Mr. Brashov meets Joe Jenkins.

_____

_____

_____

_____

_____

_____

_____

_____

_____

_____

_____

_____

Your New Language: Describing Things

This food
is bad.

To describe something, you can say:
- The hospital food is **bad.**
- The hospital food is **very bad.**
- The hospital food is **too bad to eat.**

⭐ Complete the conversations. Use these words.

strict   delicious   hot   tasteless

1.

How is your
food today?

This
hospital food is
tasteless.

2.

How is the
chicken and rice
today?

The
chicken and rice
is _____.

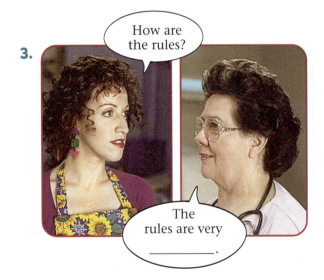

3.

How are
the rules?

The
rules are very
_____.

4.

May I
have some soup,
please?

Not
now, the soup is
too _____
to eat.

✪✪ Match.

1. How is the food?
2. Is the chicken and rice hot?
3. Does Henry come to work late?
4. Is Mr. Brashov on a strict diet?
5. Was the café busy?

a. Yes, he is on a very strict diet.
b. The food is too cold to eat.
c. Yes, the café was very busy.
d. Yes, it is too hot to eat.
e. Yes, he comes to work very late.

✪✪✪ Complete the conversation. Use these words and phrases. Write one in each blank. You may use a word or phrase more than once.

hold	too cold	very	busy
to eat	too	work	too busy
to work	very		

KATHERINE: May I leave to visit Mr. Brashov now?

JESS: Maybe later. We are very _____busy_____ now.
(1)

KATHERINE: O.K. Jess, is there a problem with the heat today?

JESS: I don't know, but it is _____ cold in here. Jamal needs to look
(2)

at the heater.

KATHERINE: Do you know where he is?

JESS: He went to buy something for the stove. When he comes back, I hope

he isn't _____ to _____ on the heater.
(3)   (4)

KATHERINE: I hope not either. We need more heat in this place. My hands are getting

_____ cold to _____ my pencil.
(5)   (6)

JESS: If we don't have heat, will we have to close the café?

KATHERINE: Not now. But if it gets worse, it will be _____ cold for the customers
(7)

_____. And it will be _____ for us _____.
(8)   (9)   (10)

JESS: O.K. Please tell me when Jamal returns from the store. Tell him that it's

_____ important that I talk with him.
(11)

✪ Put the conversation in order. Number 1 to 4.

____ MR. BRASHOV: Why? I am very hungry.

____ MR. BRASHOV: What can I eat then? The food here is tasteless!

_1_ BRENDA: Mr. Brashov, you can't eat that food.

____ BRENDA: The food is too salty.

✪✪ Put the conversation in order. Number 1 to 5.

____ ROSA: Then why aren't you eating it?

____ JESS: It smells delicious.

____ JESS: It's too hot to eat.

____ ROSA: How is the chicken and rice?

____ ROSA: It will be fine in a couple of minutes.

✪✪✪ Put the conversation in order. Number 1 to 6.

____ JESS: Please let me know when you find the problem.

____ JESS: When can you fix the fan in the kitchen? It's very hot in there.

____ JAMAL: Don't worry. I'll see what I can do. If it is too expensive to fix, I can buy a new one.

____ JAMAL: I'll go look at it now. It's a very old fan, you know.

____ JESS: Yes, I know. But I still hope you can fix it. Without a fan in the kitchen, it will be too hot to work.

____ JAMAL: O.K. As soon as I find the problem, I'll figure out how much it's going to cost.

In Your Community: Medicine Labels

Mr. Brashov has to take medicine in the hospital. Here is a label from a medicine bottle. Answer the questions about the medicine. Then tell your answers to someone.

ASPIRIN

USE: For the relief of pain from a cold, headache, flu, and fever.

DIRECTIONS: Adults: Take 1 or 2 tablets every 4 to 6 hours.

WARNING: Do not take more than 6 tablets in one day. Take with food or milk if there are stomach problems. Pregnant women **should not** take this product without permission from a doctor. Do **not** give this product to any child under 12 years of age.

POSSIBLE SIDE EFFECTS: upset stomach, heartburn, dizziness

✪ 1. What is the name of this medicine? _____

2. What is one reason people take this medicine? _____

3. How much medicine should you take at one time? _____

4. What is one possible side effect of this medicine? _____

✪✪ 1. Should you use this medicine every two hours?   YES   NO
2. Should a 5-year old child take this medicine?   YES   NO

✪✪✪ 1. If you have stomach problems, what should you do when you take this medicine?

_____

2. If you are pregnant, what should you do before you take this medicine?

_____

Look at the labels of other medicines. How are they the same as or different from the medicine label above?

Read and Write: Spotlight on Jess

Jess sends a get well card to Mr. Brashov in the hospital. Read the card very quickly to find the answers. Circle the answers.

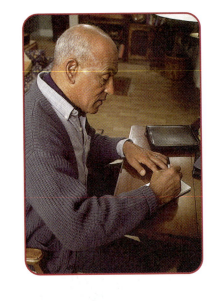

⭐ What does Jess write about?
a. the news in the neighborhood
b. how he feels about being the boss at the café
c. how Mr. Brashov feels

⭐⭐ How does Jess feel about Mr. Brashov?
a. happy　　　　　b. angry　　　　　c. nervous

⭐⭐⭐ What is the tone or feeling of the letter?
a. happy　　　　　b. sad　　　　　c. angry

Read the card again carefully.

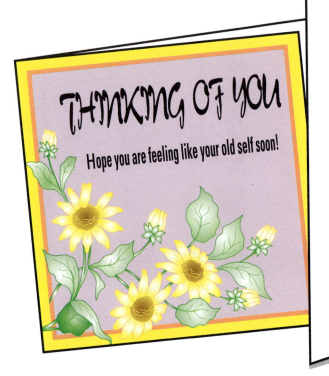

THINKING OF YOU

Hope you are feeling like your old self soon!

Dear Victor:

I was sorry to hear that you are in the hospital. Rosa tells me you had a heart attack, but that your ticker is better now. It is good that you arrived at the hospital very quickly, so doctors were able to help you.

I want to come to see you in the hospital, but the café is very busy. Maybe when you come home, we can play some chess. I really miss beating you!

I heard that your roommate, Mr. Jenkins, didn't make it. I am sorry to hear that.

Please get well soon. We all miss you. Don't worry about the café. Everything is fine. I hope to talk to you soon. If you need anything, please call me.

Fondly, Jess
P.S. Carol says hello!

Find the words in the reading. What do they mean?

⭐ To **arrive** means:
a. to come to a place
b. to leave a place
c. to talk a lot about something

⭐⭐ **Ticker** means:
a. leg　　　　　b. heart　　　　　c. stomach

⭐⭐⭐ Mr. Jenkins **didn't make it.** **Didn't make it** means:
a. He was very sick.　b. He died.　　c. He left the hospital.

Now you write a get well note to someone who is sick. Include the following information.

⭐   the name of the person you are writing to
if the person is in the hospital or at home
what is wrong with the person (flu, illness, accident)

⭐⭐   tell the person that you hope that he/she is getting better
write some news he/she might be interested in
ask if there is anything you can do while he/she is sick

⭐⭐⭐   tell what you miss about him/her
make a suggestion about what the person needs to do to get better
tell how the person can contact you if he/she needs anything

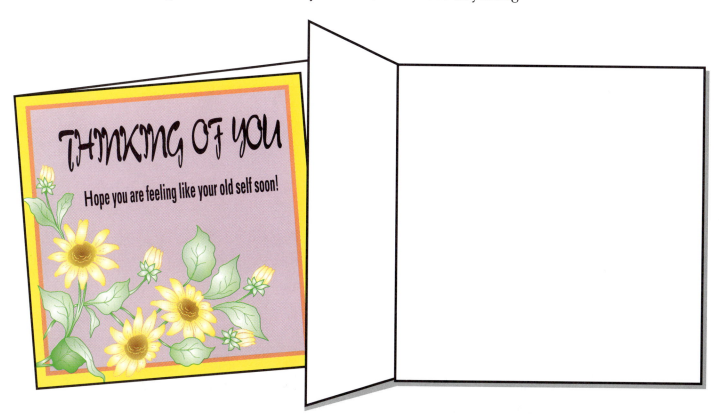

Read your note to someone. Then ask: Did you understand?
Do you have questions?

What Do You Think?

✪ Why does Mr. Brashov want to leave the hospital? Check (✓) the reasons.

☐ He misses his family.

☐ He hates the food.

☐ He doesn't like the nurses.

☐ He wants a vacation.

☐ He wants to go back to work.

✪✪ Look at the sentences below. Check (✓) I agree, I disagree, or I don't know.

	I agree.	I disagree.	I don't know.
1. Henry is too young to be the boss.	☐	☐	☐
2. Hospital rules are too strict.	☐	☐	☐
3. Mr. Brashov is a very lucky man.	☐	☐	☐

✪✪✪ Answer the following questions. Then read your sentences to someone.

1. Do you think Henry is too young to be the boss? Tell why or why not.

_____

2. Do you think hospital rules are too strict? Tell why or why not.

_____

3. Do you think Mr. Brashov is a very lucky man? Tell why or why not.

_____

Culture Clip: Hospitals

⭐ Match.

1. Friends can visit hospital patients only during visiting hours.

a.

2. Some patients eat food only from the hospital kitchen.

b.

3. Nurses explain hospital rules to patients.

c.

✪✪ Complete the paragraph about hospitals. Use these words.

medical care	nurses	doctors	patients
rules	expensive	short	city

The world of the hospital is very interesting. It is like a small ___city___. In order to
                                                                    (1)

run well, a hospital needs to have _____. The staff of a hospital is made up of many
                                        (2)

people, including _____ and _____. Everyone in the hospital works together
                      (3)   (4)

to make sure that the _____ get well as soon as possible. Patients usually stay in
                          (5)

hospitals for _____ periods of time because _____ is so _____.
                  (6)   (7)   (8)

✪✪✪ Think.

A hospital has many rules for patients and their families. List below some of the hospital
rules you know. Why do you think hospitals have so many rules? Would you add,
change, or omit any rules?

_____

_____

_____

_____

Check Your English

⭐ Write the correct word under each picture.

darkness
food tray
nurse
medicine
package
counter

1.

_____

2.

darkness

3.

_____

4.

_____

5.

_____

6.

_____

⭐⭐ Make a sentence or question from each group of words.

1. the   strict   are   hospital   rules   the   in

   The rules in the hospital are strict. OR *Are the rules in the hospital strict?*

2. diet   Mr. Brashov   on   restricted   is   a   very

   _____

3. soup   too   eat   was   to   hot   the

   _____

4. the   meatloaf   too   to   bad   is   eat

   _____

⭐⭐⭐ Finish the story. Use the words in the box. Write one word in each blank.

Mr. Brashov is in the hospital because he had a mild <u>heart attack</u>. Brenda,
                                                        (1)

the _____, takes good care of him. Jess takes charge of the _____
        (2)   (3)

while Mr. Brashov is sick. He is very _____ and everything goes well at
                                          (4)

the café. When Mr. Brashov hears this, he thinks that nobody _____
                                                                 (5)

him. Mr. Brashov shares his hospital room with another _____ named
                                                            (6)

Joe Jenkins. When Mr. Jenkins _____, Mr. Brashov feels very
                                   (7)

_____. While in the hospital, Mr. Brashov can only eat food prepared
   (8)

in the hospital because he is on a _____ diet. When Mr. Brashov feels a
                                       (9)

little better, he _____ about the _____ hospital food. After a few
                     (10)   (11)

days, Mr. Brashov goes home.

café
complains
dies
happy
heart attack
medicine
needs
nurse
organized
patient
restricted
sad
strict
tasteless
visiting hours

15 Breaking Away

In this unit you will:

- talk about likes and dislikes
- read a poster advertisement
- write a short essay about prejudice
- describe intercultural relationships

Ways to Learn

The employees at the café see Sara and Henry together often. They **infer** or **decide without all the information** that Henry and Sara are going steady. To **make inferences** means to **make decisions without all the information.**

Make Inferences

Check (✔) ways you **make inferences** in English. After reading something or listening to a conversation, I . . .

- ☐ find similarities
- ☐ find differences
- ☐ complete missing parts of conversations
- ☐ guess what will be next
- ☐ summarize
- ☐ guess people's feelings
- ☐ other: _____

On Your Own

I **make inferences** at school when . . . (check ✔)

- ☐ I read textbooks.
- ☐ I talk with classmates.
- ☐ I listen to the teacher.
- ☐ other: _____

I **make inferences** at work when . . . (check ✔)

- ☐ I talk to my supervisor.
- ☐ I talk to coworkers.
- ☐ I read manuals.
- ☐ other: _____

One problem with **making inferences** is _____

_____

Before You Watch

Look at the pictures. What do you see?

1.

2.

3.

4.

5.

6.

✪ What do you see in each picture? Write the number of the picture next to the word.

_2_ picture   ____ a family meeting

____ dinner table   ____ an angry young man

____ an unhappy young woman   ____ a young couple

✪✪ What is happening? Write the number of the picture next to the sentence.

____ Henry is talking with his parents and three other people.

____ The young woman looks unhappy.

____ Edward is looking at a picture.

_1_ Henry and a young woman are standing very close to each other.

____ Henry looks angry.

____ Henry is sitting at a dinner table with three other people.

✪✪✪ Write one question you have about each picture. Then read your questions to someone.

1. Who is the young woman? _____

2. _____

3. _____

4. _____

5. _____

6. _____

Focus For Watching   Read the questions. Then watch.

✪ 1. Who is Henry's girlfriend?
2. Who is angry with Henry?

✪✪ 1. Who tells Henry that the Graysons will not approve of him?
2. Who tells Sara's parents about going together?

✪✪✪ 1. Who would be happier if Sara were Chinese?
2. Who suggests that Henry get the parents together to talk?

After You Watch

What do you remember? Match each question with the correct picture. You can use a picture more than once.

⭐ 1. Who is Henry's girlfriend?

a. Mr. and Mrs. Chang

2. Who is angry with Henry?

b. Rosa

⭐⭐ 1. Who tells Henry that the Graysons will not approve of him?

c. Mrs. Chang

2. Who tells Sara's parents about going together?

d. Sara

⭐⭐⭐ 1. Who would be happier if Sara were Chinese?

2. Who suggests that Henry get the parents together to talk?

e. Henry

✪ Read the sentence. Circle Yes or No.

1. Henry and Sara's parents are happy.   YES   (NO)
2. The employees at Crossroads Café are
   happy about Sara and Henry.   YES   NO
3. Henry and Sara are angry with each other.   YES   NO
4. Henry has a meeting to talk about the problem.   YES   NO

✪✪ Put the sentences in order. Number 1 to 5.

_____   Henry and Sara have a fight.

_____   Henry tells his parents that he and Sara are going together.

_____   Henry goes to Sara's house for dinner.

__1__   Henry tells the Crossroads Café employees that he and Sara are going together.

_____   Henry asks the parents to come to the café for a meeting.

✪✪✪ Write the story. Use the five sentences above. Add these four sentences.
Then close the book and tell the story to someone.

• Sara tells Henry that he was rude.
• The employees are happy, but not surprised.
• Sara's parents are not happy with the news.
• Mrs. Chang tells Henry that Sara's parents will disapprove of him.

  Henry tells the Crossroads Café employees that he and Sara are going together.

_____

_____

_____

_____

_____

_____

_____

_____

_____

_____

_____

Your New Language: Talking about Likes and Dislikes

I like this place! It's really nice.

To say you like or dislike something, you can say:

- I **like** this place.
- I **don't like** this place.
- I **like** to eat here.
- I **don't like** to eat here.

⭐ Complete the conversations. Use these phrases.

that idea   that team   older women   vacant buildings

1.

Why don't you send a telegram to Sara's parents?

I like ___that idea___ !

2.

I see you have a new neighbor.

Yes. I'm glad. I don't like _____.

3.

I think she might be too old for you.

That's okay. I like _____.

4.

Do you think the Cowboys will win the Super Bowl?

I don't care. I don't like _____.

✪✪ Match.

1. I don't like our new neighbor.
2. Do you play any sports?
3. I really like Chinese food.
4. I don't like the way you behaved.
5. They don't like me!

a. I'm sorry. I'm not happy about it, either.
b. How do you know that?
c. Why not? I think she's very nice.
d. I like to play hockey.
e. I do, too. It's one of my favorite foods.

✪✪✪ Complete the conversation. Use these words or phrases. Write one in each blank. You may use a word or phrase more than once.

don't like   like   don't like to

JAMAL: What's wrong, Henry? You don't look happy.

HENRY: Sara's parents ___don't like___ me.
                                (1)

JAMAL: Why do you say that?

HENRY: They _____ the idea of their daughter going steady with
                        (2)
         a Chinese boy.

JAMAL: Have they said that to you?

HENRY: Not exactly.

JAMAL: I _____ say this to you, but maybe they _____ your long
                (3)   (4)
         hair. Or, maybe they _____ the way you behave.
                                    (5)

HENRY: You really think so?

JAMAL: I don't think so. I _____ you, Henry. I don't know why they don't.
                                    (6)
         Ask them.

⭐ Put the conversation in order. Number 1 to 3.

_____ I don't like the food there.

__1__ Let's eat at Mario's tonight.

_____ Really! Why not?

⭐⭐ Put the conversation in order. Number 1 to 4.

_____ That's a dangerous sport.

_____ Not really. I like to play hockey.

_____ That's true. But it's fun!

_____ Do you like to watch football?

⭐⭐⭐ Put the conversation in order. Number 1 to 5.

_____ That doesn't matter. Your customers come here because they like the food.

_____ I don't like the laundromat next door.

_____ You're right, but it will be noisy. Our customers like to eat in peace and quiet.

_____ Why not? At least the building won't be vacant.

_____ I know they like the food, but will they like the noise?

In Your Community: Poster Advertisement

This is the poster Linda put up on the wall at the laundromat. Answer the questions. Then tell your answers to someone.

THE FRIENDLIEST LITTLE CAFÉ IN TOWN IS RIGHT NEXT DOOR

LATIN AMERICAN, MEDITERRANEAN, AND EASTERN EUROPEAN SPECIALITIES

DAILY SPECIALS
COOKED TO ORDER USING ONLY THE FINEST AND FRESHEST INGREDIENTS

OPEN TUESDAY THROUGH SATURDAY
FROM 7:00 AM TO 3:00 PM
SUNDAY FROM 7:00 AM TO 1:00 PM
CLOSED MONDAYS

TAKE OUT AND DELIVERY SERVICE
CREDIT CARDS WELCOME

"VOTED ONE OF THE 10 BEST RESTAURANTS IN TOWN"

⭐ 1. Crossroads Café is open every day.   YES   (NO)
   2. Crossroads Café is open for breakfast.   YES   NO

⭐⭐ 1. Customers must pay in cash.   YES   NO
     2. The chef uses canned vegetables.   YES   NO

⭐⭐⭐ 1. The food is prepared in advance.   YES   NO
       2. Crossroads Café is the best restaurant in town.   YES   NO

Look at poster advertisements in your community. How are they the same as or different from the one above?

Read and Write: Spotlight on Henry

Henry writes a short essay for his English class.
Read the questions. Read Henry's essay very
quickly to find the answers. Circle the answers.

 What does Henry write about?
   a. a problem with his parents
   b. a problem with his girlfriend's parents
   c. a problem with his girlfriend

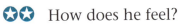 How does he feel?
   a. sad   b. confused   c. angry

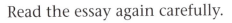 What is the tone or feeling of this essay?
   a. apologetic   b. frustrated   c. angry

Read the essay again carefully.

Henry Chang
English 1A
Jumping to Conclusions
I did something the other day that I am not very proud of. I accused some very nice people of being prejudiced.
Prejudice is a very strong word. It means having very negative feelings against a person because of his or her race, religion, or background.
I thought my girlfriend's parents didn't want us going together because I was Chinese. I was sure they didn't like me because I looked different than their little girl. This was just a feeling. I really had no proof. But, prejudice isn't always obvious.
I felt bad when my coworkers said that there might be other reasons for her parents' disapproval.
I wanted an opportunity to apologize. I asked my parents and my girlfriend's parents to come to a meeting. I had a chance to apologize. They had a chance to see that Sara and I really care about each other.

Find the word or phrase in the
reading that means the same as
the words or phrases below. Write
the correct word.

⭐ 1. dating only one person

_____

 2. opportunity

_____

⭐⭐ 1. said someone did
   something wrong

_____

 2. not approving of

_____

⭐⭐⭐ 1. evidence

_____

 2. easily seen

_____

Now you write a short essay about a situation that involved prejudice. In your essay answer the following questions.

⭐ What happened?
How did you feel?

⭐⭐ What did you say or do?
What did the other person say or do?

⭐⭐⭐ Now that you have had time to think about the situation, would you have done anything differently?

Read your essay to someone. Then ask: Did you understand?
Do you have questions?

What Do You Think?

⭐ Why do you think Sara's parents want Henry and Sara to wait? You may check (✓) more than one answer.

☐ Sara and Henry are too young.

☐ Henry is Chinese.

☐ Sara and Henry don't know each other well.

☐ Sara's parents don't like Henry.

☐ other: _____

★★ Look at the sentences below. Check (✓) I agree, I disagree, or I don't know.

	I agree.	I disagree.	I don't know.
1. Sara's parents won't want you to become involved with Sara because you are Chinese.	☐	☐	☐
2. We're old enough to know what we're doing and we're old enough to make some of our own decisions.	☐	☐	☐

✪✪✪ Answer the questions. Then read your answers to someone.

1. Do you think people should only associate with people of their own race, religion, or nationality? Tell why or why not.

_____

_____

2. Do you think teenagers are old enough to make their own decisions? Tell why or why not.

_____

_____

Culture Clip: Intercultural Relationships

✪ Match.

1. Sometimes a mother and father worry when a child chooses to marry someone from a different culture, race, or religion.

a.

2. Differences in culture, language, race, religion, and family customs may cause problems in a marriage.

b.

3. Two cultures in a marriage can enrich the lives of the children.

c.

✪✪ Complete the sentences. Write one word in each blank. Use these words.

appreciation	disagree	couple	customs
richness	adjust	decisions	cultures
concerns			

Intercultural marriages can be difficult. A __couple__ must learn not only
(1)

to _____ to a new marriage, but also to one another's _____. This
(2)   (3)

is sometimes made more difficult by the couple's families. Parents may

_____ with their childrens' _____ to marry because of race, religion,
(4)   (5)

or a concern that family _____ will be lost. Through the years these
(6)

_____ often disappear. They are replaced by an _____ for cultural
(7)   (8)

differences and the _____ these differences bring to everyone's life.
(9)

✪✪✪ Mrs. Chang tells Henry that Sara's parents won't want him to date Sara because he is Chinese. Would it bother you if someone in your family dated or married someone from another culture, race, or religion? Write your ideas. Then tell your ideas to someone.

_____

_____

_____

Check Your English

⭐ Write the correct word under each picture.

a family
   meeting

an unhappy
   young woman

a picture

an angry
   young man

dinner table

a young couple

1.

2.

3.

_____

_____

_____

4.

5.

6.

_____

a family meeting

_____

⭐⭐ Make a sentence from each group of words.

1. door   don't   the   I   neigbor   next   like

   I don't like the neighbor next door. _____

2. I   like   watch   don't   to   football

_____

3. really   food   like   at   Crossroads   the   Café   I

_____

4. eat   like   Chinese   I   restaurants   to   at

_____

⭐⭐⭐ Finish the story. Use the words in the box. Write one word in each blank.

One day at Crossroads Café Sara and Henry tell everyone that they are going

together . Everyone is happy, but not _____ . At dinner one evening
  (1)   (2)

Mrs. Chang shows Henry a _____ of a nice young Chinese girl. She
                            (3)

thinks Henry should meet this girl. Henry tells his parents about Sara. They

are not _____ . Mrs. Chang thinks Sara's parents will be unhappy because
      (4)

Henry is _____ . Sara _____ Henry to dinner to tell her parents the
     (5)   (6)

news. They are not pleased and ask Henry and Sara to _____ . Henry
                                          (7)

becomes _____ and leaves. Henry thinks the Graysons are _____ .
        (8)   (9)

The employees at Crossroads Café suggest Henry call a family _____ to
                                                   (10)

discuss the problem. Henry and Sara get back together.

angry
Chinese
invites
meeting
picture
pleased
prejudiced
sad
silly
stop
surprised
together
wait

16 The Bottom Line

In this unit you will:

- report information
- read a loan application
- write a letter
- identify roles of older people

Ways to Learn

Mr. Brashov learns to *try again* when he hears bad news from the bank. He *looks at the problem, considers solutions, asks for help* and then *tries again.*

Try and Try Again

Check (✔) the ways you *try and try again* when you have a problem learning English.

- ☐ I listen for examples.
- ☐ I look for help in books.
- ☐ I ask for help from friends and teachers.
- ☐ I read and reread, I write and rewrite.
- ☐ I make word cards to review difficult words.
- ☐ I practice with an American friend.
- ☐ I take a break, then come back to the problem.
- ☐ other: _____

On Your Own

In learning English, I have most problems with: Check (✔) one or two answers.

___ grammar   ___ pronunciation
___ spelling   ___ vocabulary
___ punctuation ___ other: _____

How will you work on these problems?

_____

_____

Before You Watch

Look at the pictures. What do you see?

1.

2.

3.

4.

5.

6.

⭐ What do you see in each picture? Write the number of the picture next to the word.

__3__ banker   _____ worried people

_____ bingo game   _____ oven part

_____ playing cards   _____ suit

⭐⭐ What is happening? Write the number of the picture next to the sentence.

__4__ Some customers play cards, knit, and sleep.

_____ Jamal is worried about something.

_____ The customers order food and play bingo.

_____ Mr. Brashov goes to a bank.

_____ Jamal is happy about something.

_____ The banker talks to Mr. Brashov about making money.

⭐⭐⭐ Write one question you have about each picture. Then read your questions to someone.

1. _Why is Rosa unhappy?_ _____

2. _____

3. _____

4. _____

5. _____

6. _____

Focus For Watching   Read the questions. Then watch.

⭐ 1. Who needs money?
2. Who gives bank loans?
3. Who brings customers to the café?

⭐⭐ 1. Who looks for an oven part?
2. Who runs a bingo game?

⭐⭐⭐ 1. Who joins a senior citizens group?
2. Who suggests making flyers to get more customers?

After You Watch

What do you remember? Match each question with the correct picture. You can use a picture more than once.

⭐ 1. Who needs money?

a. Lewis Littleton

2. Who gives bank loans?

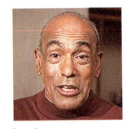

b. Jess

3. Who brings customers to the café?

c. Henry

⭐⭐ 1. Who looks for an oven part?

d. Mr. Brashov

2. Who runs a bingo game?

e. Harry

⭐⭐⭐ 1. Who joins a senior citizens group?

f. Jamal

2. Who suggests making flyers to get more customers?

★ Read the sentence. Circle Yes or No.

1. Mr. Brashov needs money to hire more employees.	YES	**(NO)**
2. The bank wants to loan Mr. Brashov money.	YES	NO
3. The people on coffee breaks order lots of food.	YES	NO
4. The lunchtime people order lots of food.	YES	NO

★★ Put the sentences in order. Number 1 to 5.

_____ Mr. Brashov needs to borrow money.

_____ Mr. Brashov doesn't need money after all.

__1__ Crossroads Café needs a new oven.

_____ Jamal finds the part for the oven.

_____ The bank won't loan Mr. Brashov money.

★★★ Write the story. Use the five sentences above. Add these three sentences. Then close the book and tell the story to someone.

• Jess brings friends from the senior citizen center for their morning coffee break.
• Mr. Littleton agrees to loan Mr. Brashov money.
• People from the senior center come to eat lunch and play bingo.

Crossroads Café needs a new oven.

_____

_____

_____

_____

_____

_____

_____

_____

_____

_____

_____

_____

_____

Your New Language: Reporting Information

The man at table one says his oatmeal is cold.

Jess, your idea is not working. Nobody is eating.

Give it a chance, Victor.

To report information, you can say:

- Jess *told* Victor to **give his idea a chance.**
- He *told* me about **Jess's idea.**

You can also repeat the person's words:

- He *says* **his oatmeal is cold.**
- Mr. Brashov *said* **Jess's idea is not working.**

⭐ Complete the conversations. Use these words.

attract   make   give   bring

1.

What did the banker tell you?

He told me to ___ *make* ___ more money.

2.

How can you attract more customers?

Katherine told me to _____ families.

3.

How can you make a good impression on a banker?

Jess told me to _____ a firm handshake.

4.

Where did all these customers come from?

I told Harry to _____ the senior citizens.

✪✪ Match.

1. Did Mr. Brashov get the loan?
2. It's quiet around here.
3. How can you attract more customers?
4. Do you need more advice about meeting with the banker?
5. Why don't we try to attract a younger crowd?

a. Katherine says people aren't eating out because of the weather.
b. Mr. Brashov says they are too noisy.
c. No, the banker told him to reduce expenses to make more money.
d. Henry said he could put flyers up all over the neighborhood.
e. No, you've already told me about things to do, things to take, and things to wear!

✪✪✪ Complete the conversation. Use these words and phrases. Write one in each blank. In some blanks more than one word or phrase is possible.

told me to   says   told me about   said
tell you about

JESS: Victor, how did it go at the bank?

MR. BRASHOV: Not very well. The bank __told me to__ attract more customers.
                                    (1)

JESS: Any ideas about how to do that?

MR. BRASHOV: Katherine _____ make the café a family-oriented restaurant.
                          (2)

JESS: What do you think of that idea?

MR. BRASHOV: I _____ I'm not going to have little kids running wild all over
                    (3)
              the place.

JESS: Any other ideas?

MR. BRASHOV: Rosa _____ a two-for-one special she saw on TV. And Henry
                        (4)
              _____ he can put flyers up around the neighborhood.
                      (5)

JESS: Let me _____ my idea.
                            (6)

MR. BRASHOV: What's that?

JESS: Bring in the senior citizens.

⭐ Put the conversation in order. Number 1 to 3.

_____ HENRY: How can he do that?

_____ JESS: Well, the bank told him to cut expenses.

__1__ JESS: The bank told Victor to make more money.

⭐⭐ Put the conversation in order. Number 1 to 5.

_____ HENRY: Expenses like what?

_____ HENRY: So we don't have to worry about our jobs?

_____ JAMAL: Mr. Brashov said he could cut food, utilities, or supplies.

_____ JAMAL: The bank told Mr. Brashov to reduce expenses.

_____ JAMAL: I'm not so sure. Jess said Mr. Brashov could lay off employees.

⭐⭐⭐ Put the conversation in order. Number 1 to 8.

_____ ROSA: First of all, Henry told him to go after a younger crowd.

_____ JESS: Tell me about them.

_____ JESS: Rosa, how can Victor make money when people buy one and get one free!

_____ ROSA: We've made several suggestions to Mr. Brashov about how to attract more customers.

_____ ROSA: He said he's not going to buy high chairs or have little kids spilling milk and breaking glasses. So I told him about a two-for-one special I saw on TV.

_____ ROSA: Right. Then Katherine told him to make it a family-oriented restaurant.

_____ JESS: And Victor said they're too noisy. Right?

_____ JESS: What did Victor think about that?

In Your Community: Loan Applications

This is the application form that Mr. Brashov filled out for a loan. Answer the questions about the information on the form. Then share your answers with someone.

First Federal

Business Loan Application

Business Name	Tax I.D. Number
Crossroads Café	

Business Location (Street Address)	Telephone Number
2950 West 53rd St.	(217) 555-2345

Mailing Address	Number of Employees	Annual Sales
Middletown, IL 12345	4	$ 235,000

Type of Ownership	☐ Limited Liability Company ☒ Sole Proprietorship ☐ Partnership ☐ Corporation ☐ S Corp	Number of Years in Operation 1 year
		Present Management Since Opening

Loan Request   *All Loans Are Subject to a Loan Fee

Loan Amount Requested	Use of Loan Proceeds
$3,000.00	Purchase new equipment (oven)

Sources of Repayment (Alimony, child support, or separate maintainance income need not be revealed unless you want it considered as a basis for repaying this obligation.)

A.   B.

Collateral Description	Value	Source/Date	Rate - Bank Use Only
existing equipment	$8,000.00	8/95	

Existing Indebtedness — Furnish the following information on loans and obligations which are currently outstanding.
* Please check any existing indebtedness that you plan to pay off with this loan.

Payable To	*✓	Original Amount	Original Date	Current Balance	Interest Rate	Maturity Date	Monthly Payment	Collateral	Current ✓	Past Due ✓
Larson's Appliances		$12,000	8/95	$9,900	8 ½%	8/2001	$300	equipment		

Business Information

What Product or Service Does Your Business Offer?
food - restaurant

What Geographic Area Does Your Business Serve?	Will Your Current Facility Be Adequate for the Next Five Years?
downtown	☒ Yes ☐ No

If You Lease Your Facility, Please Provide

Name of Your Landlord	Address	Lease Expiration Date 8/98
Seymour Schuster	475 N. Main	Monthly Lease Pmt $ $1,000

Are All Your Business Taxes Current? (Including Payroll Taxes) ☒ Yes ☐ No	If No, Please Explain	Have You Had an IRS or State Audit in the Last 3 Years? ☐ Yes ☒ No

Please List Your Major Trade Suppliers

Name	Address	Phone No.	% of Purchases
ABC Meat Company	147 Park St.	555-2424	25%
Alan Brothers Coffee	29 Glover Ave.	555-8724	20%
United Grocers	18 Birch St.	555-3982	55%

General Information

Who Owns the Business Name	Title	Percentage of Ownership
Victor Brashov	Owner	100%

Your Insurance Company/Agent	Address	Phone No.
First Insurance of America	942 Flower St.	555-2314

Your Accountant/Bookkeeper	Address	Phone No.
self		

Where Do You Currently Bank?	What services do you use?
First Federal	checking and savings accounts, loan

The statements made herein are true, and represent a total disclosure of all the information requested as of this date. Applicant authorizes all references contained herein, as well as any other source of information pertaining to the applicant's credit worthiness, to disclose such information to First Interstate Bank or its agent. I further authorize any First Interstate Bank to provide information concerning applicant's credit relationship to credit reporting agencies or other creditors.

Name of Applicant	Victor Brashov
Title	owner, Crossroads Café
Signature	Victor Brashov	Date April 16, 1997

FOR BANK USE

Received By	Date	Action Taken ☐ Approved ☐ Declined ☐ Rejected	Date
Branch			
Forwarded to	Date	Customer Notified ☐ In Person ☐ Telephone ☐ Letter	Date
CBC/CLO			
CBC/CLO Officer Name		Branch Notified (if referred) ☐ Telephone ☐ cc Letter	Date

---

✪ 1. What is the loan amount requested? _____

2. Does Mr. Brashov own or lease the café? How do you know? _____

✪✪ 1. Does Mr. Brashov's business have any debts? _____

2. To whom does Mr. Brashov owe money? How much does he owe? _____

✪✪✪ If Mr. Brashov doesn't pay back the loan, what will the bank get?

_____

_____

Now get a loan application from a bank in your community. How is it the same as or different from the one above?

Read and Write: Spotlight on Mr. Brashov

Read the questions. Read Mr. Brashov's letter to his brother very quickly to find the answers. Circle the answers.

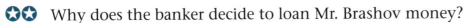

⭐ What does Mr. Brashov write about?
  a. employee problems
  b. money problems
  c. problems with Jess

⭐⭐ Why does the banker decide to loan Mr. Brashov money?
  a. He thinks the café has a lot of customers.
  b. He thinks Mr. Brashov is a hard worker.
  c. He likes Mr. Brashov.

⭐⭐⭐ What is the tone or feeling of this letter?
  a. disappointed   b. worried   c. relieved

Read the letter again carefully.

Dear Nicolae,

  Another interesting week. The oven isn't working well. Jamal said we need a new heat regulator, but the oven is so old we can't get parts. A new oven means borrowing money from the bank.

  Well, the banker said increase profits or no loan. He said that I should cut expenses or lay off employees. Of course, I don't want any of my employees to lose their jobs. Henry said the café needs more customers, so Jess brought his senior citizens group. They were here for their weekly bingo game when the banker showed up. It was lunchtime. Everybody was eating. The banker was impressed. He said he could give me the loan.

  Again Jamal saved the day. He showed up with the part. He found it in a junkyard. Now I don't need the loan.

  Love, Victor

Find the word in the reading. What does it mean? Circle the answer.

⭐ **Lay off** means employees
  a. get a raise   b. get a vacation   c. lose their jobs

⭐⭐ When you **get a loan**, you
  a. borrow money   b. give money   c. return money

⭐⭐⭐ The banker was **impressed**, because he
  a. couldn't see   b. liked what he saw   c. didn't like what he saw

Now you continue Mr. Brashov's letter. Give the following information.

⭐ Why did the senior citizens first come to the café?
Did they help Mr. Brashov make more money?
Why or why not?

⭐⭐ Who did Henry want to attract as customers?
What did Mr. Brashov think of that idea?
Who did Katherine want to attract as customers?
What did Mr. Brashov think of that idea?

⭐⭐⭐ What expenses does Mr. Brashov say he can cut?
How does he feel about that?

Read your letter to someone. Then ask: Did you understand?
Do you have questions?

What Do You Think?

⭐ Mr. Brashov needs to make more profit. What do you think he should do first, second, third? Number the sentences 1 to 3.

_____ He should find more customers.

_____ He should lay off employees.

_____ He should buy cheaper meat and day-old bread.

⭐⭐ Look at the sentences below. Check (✓) I agree, I disagree, or I don't know.

	I agree.	I disagree.	I don't know.
1. You are only as old as you feel.	☐	☐	☐
2. His thinking is too old-fashioned. What do you expect from somebody who's over forty?	☐	☐	☐
3. Never underestimate the power of senior citizens.	☐	☐	☐

⭐⭐⭐ Answer the questions. Then read your answers to someone.

1. Are you only as old as you feel? Tell why or why not.

_____

2. Do you think people over forty are old-fashioned? Tell why or why not.

_____

3. Do you think senior citizens have a lot of political power? Tell why or why not.

_____

Culture Clip: Aging

⭐ Match.

1. Some older people live with their children and have clearly defined family roles.

a.

2. Some older people don't live with their children.

b.

3. Some older people try to stay active.

c.

4. Some do volunteer work, helping others.

d.

⭐⭐ Complete the sentences. Write one word in each blank. Use these words.

active	help	roles	children
library	time	grandpas	older
volunteer			

In some cultures, older people have clearly defined ___roles___ within the family. But in the
(1)

United States, _____ people often live away from their _____. Their lives may take
(2) (3)

different paths. They may be very _____, using their free _____ for activities like
(4) (5)

backpacking or mountain climbing. Others may _____ their time to _____ others.
(6) (7)

They may work at places like a child care center, a rest home, a _____, or a school. Grandmas
(8)

and _____ are always needed, and doing something for somebody else keeps them going.
(9)

⭐⭐⭐ Think.

Jess says, "Some days I feel old." Are there things he can do so he
doesn't feel old? Write your ideas. Then tell your ideas to someone.

_____

_____

Check Your English

⭐ Write the correct word under each picture.

suit
cards
bingo game
worried people
oven part
banker

1.
_____

2.
_____

3.
_____

4.
_____suit_____

5.
_____

6.
_____

⭐⭐ Make a sentence from each group of words.

1. money   told   more   Mr. Littleton   make   Mr. Brashov   to

   Mr. Littleton told Mr. Brashov to make more money.

2. told   Rosa   special   about   him   two-for-one   a

   _____

3. says   people   young   Mr. Brashov   noisy   too   are

   _____

4. bread   won't   said   buy   he   Mr. Brashov   day-old

   _____

⭐⭐⭐ Finish the story. Use the words in the box. Write one word in each blank.

   The stove at Crossroads Café isn't __working__ (1), and it is so old that Mr. Brashov can't get _____ (2) for it. He needs money to buy a new stove. He _____ (3) to a bank to apply for a loan. The _____ (4), Mr. Littleton, tells Mr. Brashov that he is spending too much _____ (5). The café isn't making enough money. It needs to make _____ (6) money. It needs more customers.

   Jess _____ (7) to help. First, he brings senior _____ (8) to the café for their coffee break. They don't _____ (9) food. Then, he brings them for their weekly bingo _____ (10). They order lunch. Mr. Littleton sees all the _____ (11) with their orders and decides he can _____ (12) Mr. Brashov money. But Jamal finds the stove part, so Mr. Brashov doesn't need a loan after all.

bank
banker
cards
citizens
customers
game
goes
loan
money
more
order
parts
time
wants
working

17 United We Stand

In this unit you will:

- make complaints
- ask for help
- read a rental lease
- write a letter of complaint
- identify tenant and landlord rights and responsibilities

Ways to Learn

Rosa had **to read** her apartment lease to **know** her tenant rights. The lease is a long and difficult document. Rosa doesn't have to understand every word. She has to read for meaning to understand the message.

Read For Meaning

Check (✓) ways you **get meaning** from difficult documents.

- ☐ I read headings—words in bold or large type.
- ☐ I scan the page—look for specific information.
- ☐ I skim the page—look for general information or the main idea.
- ☐ I circle or underline important words.
- ☐ I guess meaning.
- ☐ I look for word endings (*ed, es, ing . . .*).
- ☐ I look for time words (*before, after, yesterday . . .*).
- ☐ I look up some words in a bilingual dictionary.
- ☐ other: _____

On Your Own

Circle the documents you will try to **read for meaning.**

apartment lease	job manual
loan application	job memo
job application	business letter

How will you read for meaning in the future?

_____

_____

_____

_____

Before You Watch

Look at the pictures. What do you see?

1.

2.

3.

4.

5.

6.

✪ What do you see in each picture? Write the number of the picture next to the word.

_2_ pipe   ___ signs

___ tenants' meeting   ___ faucet

___ check   ___ letter

✪✪ What is happening? Write the number of the picture next to the sentence.

___ The tenants are having a meeting about their housing problems.

___ Jamal is fixing the leaky pipe in Rosa's bathroom.

___ The tenants have made protest signs.

_1_ Rosa is having problems with her faucet.

___ Rosa is writing a letter of complaint to her building manager.

___ Rosa is giving her rent check to the building manager.

✪✪✪ Write one question you have about each picture. Then read your questions to someone.

1. What is Rosa going to do about the water problem?

2. _____

3. _____

4. _____

5. _____

6. _____

Focus For Watching   Read the questions. Then watch.

✪ 1. Who has a leaky pipe?
   2. Who tries to fix the broken pipe?
   3. Who helps make the signs at the tenants' meeting?

✪✪ 1. Who brings the TV reporter to the meeting?
    2. Who asks for the rent check?

✪✪✪ 1. Who suggests that Rosa have the tenants' meeting?
     2. Who doesn't think Rosa should write the letter?

After You Watch

What do you remember? Match each question with the correct picture. You can use a picture more than once.

⭐ 1. Who has a leaky pipe?

a. Henry

2. Who tries to fix the broken pipe?

b. Rosa

3. Who helps make the signs at the tenants' meeting?

c. Mr. Brashov

⭐⭐ 1. Who brings the TV reporter to the meeting?

d. Jamal

2. Who asks for the rent check?

e. Katherine

⭐⭐⭐ 1. Who suggests that Rosa have the tenants' meeting?

f. Building Manager

2. Who doesn't think Rosa should write the letter?

g. Jess

★ Read the sentence. Circle Yes or No.
1. Rosa lives in a new apartment building.   YES   (NO)
2. Rosa is happy with her apartment.   YES   NO
3. Rosa writes a letter to the building manager.   YES   NO
4. The tenants meet to talk about the problems.   YES   NO
5. The owner wants to fix the problems.   YES   NO

★★ Put the sentences in order. Number 1 to 5.

_____ The tenants hold a meeting to discuss what to do about the housing problems.

_____ Jamal goes to Rosa's apartment to try to fix Rosa's water problem.

_____ The owner comes to the meeting to hear the complaints.

_1_ Rosa has a plumbing problem.

_____ Rosa writes a letter to the building manager describing all the problems.

★★★ Write the story. Use the five sentences above. Add these three sentences.
Then close the book and tell the story to someone.
• Rosa calls the building manager, but he doesn't answer.
• Rosa is invited to talk with the other owners about the problems.
• A TV reporter comes to the meeting to write a story about the problems.

Rosa has a plumbing problem.

_____

_____

_____

_____

_____

_____

_____

_____

_____

_____

_____

_____

Your New Language: Making Complaints

I'm from the property management company. We haven't received your rent yet.

I have some problems in my apartment. My pipe leaks. The tile is cracked. We need some repairs done. When can you fix these things?

To make a housing complaint you need to:

- tell about the problem

  The stove doesn't work.

  My pipe leaks.

  My faucet is dripping.

  The tile is cracked.

  The drapes are torn.

- ask for help

  We need some repairs done.

  When can you fix these things?

★ Complete Rosa's messages to the landlord. Use these words.

air conditioner   stove   sink   light switch
garbage disposal   window

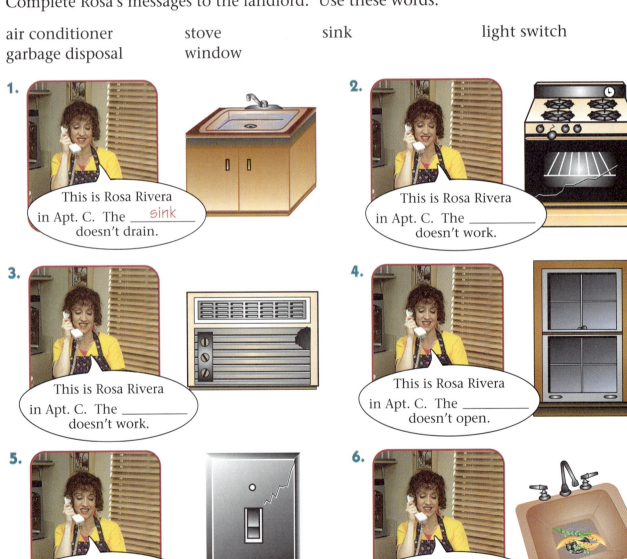

1. This is Rosa Rivera in Apt. C. The _____sink_____ doesn't drain.

2. This is Rosa Rivera in Apt. C. The _____ doesn't work.

3. This is Rosa Rivera in Apt. C. The _____ doesn't work.

4. This is Rosa Rivera in Apt. C. The _____ doesn't open.

5. This is Rosa Rivera in Apt. C. The _____ doesn't work.

6. This is Rosa Rivera in Apt. C. The _____ doesn't work.

✪✪ Match.
1. What's the problem?
2. When can you fix it?
3. My faucet is dripping.
4. I have some problems in my apartment.
5. The refrigerator doesn't work.

a. In the bathroom or in the kitchen?
b. What kind of problems?
c. The garbage disposal doesn't work.
d. Is it plugged in?
e. I'll come over around 11:00 A.M. tomorrow.

✪✪✪ Complete the conversation. Use these words or phrases. Write one in each blank.

leaks   is peeling   need some repairs   rent check
doesn't drain   is broken   have problems   water pressure
when can you

BUILDING MANAGER: I'm from the property management company. I haven't received

your _____rent check_____ yet.
                      (1)

ROSA: I know. I _____ done.
                              (2)

BUILDING MANAGER: What kind of repairs?

ROSA: I _____ with the _____ in my
                      (3)   (4)
                bathroom, the toilet _____ and the paint
                                           (5)
                _____. The sink in the kitchen _____
                      (6)   (7)
                and the garbage disposal _____. _____
                                               (8)   (9)
                fix these things?

BUILDING MANAGER: I don't know. I'll need to get back to you.

ROSA: I'll pay the rent when you can repair these things.

★ Put the conversation in order. Number 1 to 4.

____	MR. BRASHOV:	Did you call your landlord?
____	ROSA:	I'm sorry. I didn't have any water in my apartment this morning. My plumbing doesn't work.
____	ROSA:	Yes, but he wasn't home.
1	MR. BRASHOV:	Rosa, why are you late?

★★ Put the conversation in order. Number 1 to 5.

____	ROSA:	Thanks, Jamal. I really appreciate it.
____	JAMAL:	You have a water problem. Not much pressure in the pipes.
____	JAMAL:	You're welcome. But you really should tell your landlord about this soon.
____	ROSA:	Can you fix it?
____	JAMAL:	I'll do my best.

★★★ Put the conversation in order. Number 1 to 7.

____	LANDLORD:	O.K. I'll see you at 10:00. O.K.?
____	LANDLORD:	What's the problem?
____	ROSA:	This is Rosa Rivera, your tenant in Apartment C. I have a problem in my apartment.
____	LANDLORD:	Well, I'll need to come and look at the problems first. What's a good day this week?
____	ROSA:	Yes. Thank you.
____	ROSA:	Actually, I have several problems. My faucet leaks in the bathroom, the tile is cracking, the paint is peeling and the sink doesn't drain. When can you fix these things?
____	ROSA:	How about tomorrow? I'm home in the morning.

In Your Community: Rental Leases

This is the rental lease that Rosa signed for her apartment. Answer the questions about her lease. Then tell your answers to someone.

This lease entered into this _15th_ day of _November_, 199_6_ by and between _Robert Ruiz_, (Landlord) and _Rosa Rivera_, (Tenant), witnesseth that the LANDLORD above leases to the TENANT above, the premises located at _493 Main St., Apt. C, Middletown, IL_. The term of this lease shall be _12 months_, beginning at _12:00 P.M._ on _December 1_, 199_6_ and ending at _12:00 P.M._, on _November 30_, 199_7_.
Premises shall be occupied by the following named persons:

Rosa Rivera	_26_		
Name	Age	Name	Age

Rent is due in advance on the _1st_ day of each and every month at $_400.00_ per month, beginning on the _1st_ day of _December_, 199_6_. TENANT has deposited with LANDLORD, as a security deposit, the sum of $_400.00_. LANDLORD may withhold from the security deposit to: 1) remedy tenant default in the payment of rent, 2) to repair damages to premises caused by TENANT, 3) to clean premises upon termination of tenancy. TENANT shall pay for all utilities, services and charges, except _water_, and _trash_. Without LANDORD's prior written consent, no bird, animal, reptile, fish, waterbed or other liquid-filled furniture shall be kept or allowed in or about said premises. TENANT has inspected the premises, furnishings and equipment, and has found them to be satisfactory. All plumbing, heating and electrical systems are operative and satisfactory. Tenant is subject to a late charge fee of $_25.00_, starting on the 1st day of each month after _6:00 P.M._. The undersigned TENANT acknowledges having read and understood the above, and receipt of duplicate.

Robert Ruiz
LANDLORD

Rosa Rivera
TENANT

_____
TENANT

⭐ 1. Rosa lives at _____.

2. Her rent is $_____.

3. The landlord's name is _____.

⭐⭐ 1. The rent must be paid on _____. She is charged a late fee of $_____ if it is _____ days late.

2. The _____ has to pay for the electricity.

3. Can the landlord keep the security deposit? _____

4. What can her landlord use her security deposit for? _____

✪✪✪ 1. What is she not allowed to have in her apartment? _____

2. Do you think Rosa should have signed this lease? Tell why or why not.

_____

Look at a copy of a rental lease. How is the lease the same as or different from the one above?

Read and Write: Spotlight on Rosa

Read the questions. Read Rosa's letter of complaint very quickly to find the answers. Circle the answers.

⭐ What does Rosa write about?
  a. problems with her apartment only
  b. problems in her apartment and in her building

⭐⭐ How does she feel about her apartment?
  a. happy   b. unhappy   c. satisfied

⭐⭐⭐ What is the tone or feeling of her letter?
  a. apologetic   b. cheerful   c. serious

Read the letter again carefully.

Apt. # C

Dear Building Manager,

I am writing this letter to complain about the condition of my apartment and the basic services in the

apartment building. I have tried to call you many times, but I always get your answering machine.

My bathroom faucet has no water pressure, the elevator doesn't work well, and there is garbage in the

alley. As a tenant who pays her rent on time, I think you should take care of these problems. My lease

guarantees these basic services. I would like to talk to you soon about this. I am not happy. If I don't

hear from you by Friday, I will contact the renter's association. Please call me. Thank you.

Sincerely, Rosa Rivera

Find the words in the reading. What do they mean? Circle the answer.

⭐ 1. **basic services** means:
  a. water   b. gas   c. electricity   d. all of these

 2. **alley** means:
  a. an aisle   b. small street behind   c. walkway in the
                          or beside a building   front of a house

⭐⭐ 1. **to pay on time** means:
  a. to pay early   b. to pay late   c. to pay when one
                                                        is supposed to

 2. **get your answering machine** means:
  a. the machine is   b. the answering machine   c. the telephone is
     working   answers the call   not working

⭐⭐⭐ 1. **to complain about something** means:
  a. to criticize   b. to agree with   c. to be satisfied with

 2. **condition** means:
  a. the state of   b. the qualifications   c. health
     something

Now you write a letter of complaint. Include this information in your letter.

⭐ your address
the date
the name of the person you are writing to
the problem(s)
what you want the person to do

⭐⭐ how long you have had the problem(s)
what your lease guarantees

⭐⭐⭐ a deadline by which you expect action
what you will do if there is no response

Read your entry to someone. Then ask: Did you understand?
Do you have questions?

What Do You Think?

⭐ What do you think Rosa should do 1st, 2nd, 3rd, 4th? Number the pictures 1 to 4.

____   __1__   ____   ____

⭐⭐ Look at the sentences below. Check (✓) I agree, I disagree, or I don't know.

	I agree.	I disagree.	I don't know.

1. You sound like you're apologizing for sending a letter. Be more aggressive. ☐ ☐ ☐

2. You write that letter, you'll lose that apartment. ☐ ☐ ☐

3. Well, maybe you can't fight this alone, but if you organize all the tenants together who knows what you can do. ☐ ☐ ☐

⭐⭐⭐ Answer the questions. Then read your answers to someone.

1. Do you think Rosa should be more aggressive in her letter? Tell why or why not.

_____

2. Do you think she will lose her apartment if she complains? Tell why or why not.

_____

3. Do you think she should organize the tenants? Tell why or why not.

_____

Culture Clip: Tenant and Landlord Rights and Responsibilities

⭐ Match.

1. tenant abuse

2. landlord abuse

3. unsafe

4. mediation

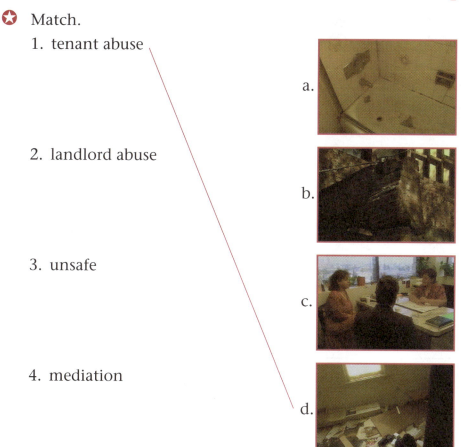

a.

b.

c.

d.

⭐⭐ Complete the sentences. Use these words.

problem   responsible   responsibility   tenants   owner

People who own a home are <u>responsible</u> for its upkeep. But when people
                                    (1)

live in places owned by others, this _____ is shared by landlord and
                                          (2)

renter. _____ must tell the building _____ or manager when
            (3)   (4)

a _____ develops.
      (5)

⭐⭐⭐ Think.

Rosa took several steps to solve her rental problem. Do you think if a rental
problem is serious, and not taken care of within a reasonable period of time,
a renter should request legal help? Why or why not? Write your ideas.
Then tell your ideas to someone.

_____

_____

_____

Check Your English

⭐ Write the correct word under each picture.

tenants'
  meeting

signs

letter

faucet

check

a pipe

1.

_____

2.

_____

3.

_____

4.

_____

5.

tenants' meeting

6.

_____

⭐⭐ Make a sentence or question from each group of words.

1. drain   sink   doesn't   the

_____

2. the   doesn't   window   open

_____

3. and   pipe   cracked   leaks   the   tile   the   is

_____

4. is   my   again   dripping   faucet

_____

⭐⭐⭐ Finish the story. Use the words in the box. Write one word in each blank.

Rosa has a __plumbing__ problem. Rosa calls the building _____, but he
          (1)   (2)
doesn't answer. Jamal _____ to stop by and take a look at Rosa's
                    (3)
_____ problem. Rosa _____ a letter to the building manager
  (4)   (5)
describing all the problems. There are several problems. The problems
include: lack of water, unreliable _____ and a _____ alley. The
                                    (6)   (7)
_____ hold a _____ to discuss what to do about the housing
  (8)   (9)
problems. A TV _____ comes to the meeting to write a story about the
              (10)
_____. The owner comes to the meeting to hear the _____. Rosa is
  (11)   (12)
invited to talk with the other _____ about the problems.
                                (13)

clean
complaints
dirty
elevators
manager
meeting
noise
offers
owners
plumbing
problems
reporter
tenants
water
writes

18 Opportunity Knocks

In this unit you will:

- compare things
- read a business card
- write a cover letter
- Identify laws that protect workers

Ways to Learn

Jamal is *open to learning* and wants to try a new opportunity. *Being open* is important for learning a new language. *To be open to learning* means to *try new opportunities.*

Be Open to Learning

Check (✔) how you are *open to learning* English.

- ☐ I listen to suggestions for improvement.
- ☐ I ask for help.
- ☐ I see my mistakes.
- ☐ I use what I learn in class or from textbooks.
- ☐ I cooperate with classmates or coworkers.
- ☐ I start conversations with English speakers.
- ☐ I go to events where people speak English.
- ☐ other: _____

On Your Own

I can be more *open to learn* if _____
_____

List 2 new ways you were *open to learning* last week.

1. _____
   _____

2. _____
   _____

Before You Watch

Look at the pictures. What do you see?

1.

2.

3.

4.

5.

6.

✪ What do you see in each picture? Write the number of the picture next to the word.

__2__ angry person   ____ cellular phone

____ computer   ____ jukebox

____ hard hat   ____ happy people

✪✪ What is happening? Write the number of the picture next to the sentence.

____ Jamal works on a computer.

____ Mr. Brashov is angry at Jamal.

__1__ Two men deliver a jukebox to Crossroads Café.

____ Jamal talks to a man at a construction site.

____ A customer talks on his cellular phone.

____ Jamal and Mr. Brashov are very happy.

✪✪✪ Write one question you have about each picture. Then read your questions to someone.

1. Why is Mr. Brashov happy? _____

2. _____

3. _____

4. _____

5. _____

6. _____

Focus For Watching   Read the questions. Then watch.

✪ 1. Who owns a construction company?
   2. Who leaves his job at the café?

✪✪ 1. Who fixes the jukebox?
    2. Who gives Jamal an envelope of money?

✪✪✪ 1. Who is the foreman at the construction site?
     2. Who sees something wrong on the computer?

After You Watch

What do you remember? Match each question with the correct picture. You can use a picture more than once.

⭐ 1. Who owns a construction company?

a. Rick Marshall

2. Who leaves his job at the café?

b. Jamal

⭐⭐ 1. Who fixes the jukebox?

2. Who gives Jamal an envelope of money?

c. Joe Cassidy

⭐⭐⭐ 1. Who is the foreman at the construction site?

d. Mr. Brashov

2. Who sees something wrong on the computer?

✪ Read the sentence. Circle Yes or No.

1. Jamal has a new handyman job.   YES   (NO)
2. Everyone likes the music on the jukebox.   YES   NO
3. Jamal has a problem with his new boss.   YES   NO
4. Jamal comes back to work at Crossroads Café.   YES   NO

✪✪ Put the sentences in order. Number 1 to 4.

____ Jamal quits his engineering job.

____ Jamal becomes unhappy about the materials Mr. Marshall uses in his buildings.

__1__ One day a customer named Mr. Marshall comes into the café.

____ Jamal leaves Crossroads Café to work as an engineer.

✪✪✪ Write the story. Use the four sentences above. Add these four sentences. Then close the book and tell the story to someone.

- He then goes back to his handyman job at the café.
- Mr. Marshall gets angry and wants Jamal to do something wrong.
- Mr. Marshall owns a construction business and offers Jamal a job.
- He wants Mr. Marshall to stop using old building materials.

One day a customer named Mr. Marshall comes into the café. Mr. Marshall owns a construction business and offers Jamal a job.

_____

_____

_____

_____

_____

_____

_____

_____

_____

_____

_____

_____

_____

Your New Language: Comparing Things

We need more customers on Saturday and Sunday.

I don't know why, but business is always slower on the weekend.

To compare people, places, or things you can say:

- Mr. Brashov is big**er than** Rosa.
- Henry is young**er than** Jess.
- The furniture is **more expensive than** the refrigerator.

⭐ Complete the conversations. Use these words.

busier   warmer   nicer   safer

1.

How do you like the jukebox?

It's _____nicer_____ than the one my friend has.

2.

Why did you buy a jukebox?

I want the café to be _____ than it is now.

3.

Our buildings are fine.

No, they're not. People will be working there. Your buildings need to be a lot _____ than they are now.

4.

How is the heat in the dining room?

Much better, thanks. It is much _____ now than it was this morning.

✪✪ Match.

1. How is business at the café on the weekends?

2. This kitchen is too small.

3. Does Henry like his job?

4. When do you like to walk?

a. Yes, I know. We need to make it bigger than it is now.

b. Yes, but he is more interested in music.

c. Anytime. But it is safer to walk during the day than at night.

d. O.K. But it is busier during the week.

✪✪✪ Complete the conversation. Write one word in each blank. Use these words.

newer	more	problem	safer
cheaper	stronger	later	building
old			

JAMAL: Can we talk for a minute? I think we may have a ___problem___.
(1)

MR. MARSHALL: I'm writing a report right now. Can we talk _____?
(2)

JAMAL: No, I think this is _____ important. It's about your
(3)

_____ materials. Why aren't you using _____
(4)   (5)

materials? These are too _____. You need to replace them.
(6)

MR. MARSHALL: We don't need to replace them. They are fine.

JAMAL: No they aren't. The beams have to be much _____ to support
(7)

the weight of the buildings. Aren't you concerned about the people

who will be working there? You need a _____ building than
(8)

those beams will give you.

MR. MARSHALL: Of course, I'm concerned. But these _____ materials work
(9)
just as well.

⭐ Put the conversation in order. Number 1 to 4.

_____ MR. BRASHOV: Good. I hope we stay busy.

_____ KATHERINE: Not bad. It was busier than yesterday.

_____ KATHERINE: I do, too. I hope we have more customers tomorrow than we did today.

__1__ MR. BRASHOV: Hello. How was business this morning?

⭐⭐ Put the conversation in order. Number 1 to 4.

_____ JAMAL: That's not my problem. I am a better engineer than a jukebox repairman.

_____ JAMAL: I am not sure. I don't know what is wrong with it.

_____ MR. BRASHOV: When you're finished with the toaster can you look at the jukebox?

_____ MR. BRASHOV: Can you fix the toaster today?

⭐⭐⭐ Put the conversation in order. Number 1 to 7.

_____ MR. BRASHOV: I don't think so. But I'm not sure. Can you look at these records for me?

_____ HENRY: Put in some different records. Rock music is more popular than any other music. Do you have any rock music here?

_____ HENRY: I think it's worse than the music we heard yesterday.

_____ MR. BRASHOV: That's O.K. You know your music, Henry. I'll try anything you say.

_____ MR. BRASHOV: What can I do to make it better?

_____ MR. BRASHOV: Henry, how do you like the music in the jukebox today?

_____ HENRY: Sure. If we don't have any rock music, you might have to buy some.

In Your Community: Business Cards

Rick Marshall gives a business card to Jamal. Read the card and then answer the questions. Then tell your answers to someone.

Rick Marshall
President
Regal Engineering and Construction
818 Main Street
Middletown, IL 12345
(217) 555-1084 (phone)
(217) 555-0947 (fax)

Commercial and Residential Construction

- Engineering Services
- New Construction
- Home Improvements
- Additions
- Fully Insured
- Free Estimates

⭐ 1. What is the name of Mr. Marshall's company? _____

2. Where is Mr. Marshall's company located? _____

⭐⭐ 1. Does Mr. Marshall's company build offices?   YES   NO

2. Does Mr. Marshall's company build roads?   YES   NO

⭐⭐⭐ 1. You find a house for sale that you want to buy. Would you contact Mr. Marshall to find out how much it costs? Why or why not?

_____

_____

2. You hire Mr. Marshall's company to build a room for you. One of his workers gets hurt while working on the room. Do you have to pay his medical bills? Why or why not?

_____

_____

3. You want Mr. Marshall to make some repairs on your house. He gives you an estimate on how much the repairs are going to cost. How much do you have to pay for this estimate?

_____

_____

Look at other business cards. How are they the same as or different from Mr. Marshall's business card?

Read and Write: Spotlight on Jamal

Jamal writes a letter to an engineering firm about a job. Read Jamal's letter very quickly to find the answers.

⭐ What does Jamal write about?
a. He wants information about an engineering problem.
b. He wants to go back to engineering school.
c. He wants an engineering job.

⭐⭐ How does Jamal feel about this job?
a. worried   b. nervous   c. hopeful

⭐⭐⭐ What is the tone or feeling of this letter?
a. confident   b. sad   c. angry

Now read the letter again carefully.

Find the words in the reading. What do they mean? Circle the answers.

17 Cummings St. Apt. 2
Middletown, IL 12345

1 Mr. Brandon F. Fine, President
Fine Engineering Company
1220 95th Street - Room 3111
Middletown, IL 12345

2 Dear Mr. Fine:

3 I would like to be considered for the position of "Hydraulic Engineer" as advertised in the newspaper. I believe that I have both the education and experience to handle the responsibilities of this job.

My résumé is enclosed for your review. As you can see, I have had many years of experience in the engineering field, both in Egypt and here in the United States. I worked on many hydraulics projects, so I am familiar with the systems. I am confident that I could be of great assistance to your company.

I would like the opportunity to further discuss this engineering position with you. If you need any information or would like to schedule an interview, please contact me at (217) 555-7890.

4 Sincerely yours,

Jamal Al-Jibali

5 Jamal Al-Jibali

⭐ To **review** means:
a. to write a report
b. to look at something
c. to apply for a job

⭐⭐ A **position** is:
a. a job
b. the amount of money a person earns
c. the amount of time spent in a job

⭐⭐⭐ A **résumé** is:
a. a short list of a person's education and job experience
b. a letter that a person writes to a business
c. the number of years of job experience a person has

Now you write a letter to someone about a job you are interested in. Fill in parts 1–5 like Jamal's letter and answer the following questions:

⭐ 1. What job are you interested in?
2. Where did you find out about the job?

✪✪ 1. What kind of education and training do you have?
2. How many years of work experience do you have?

✪✪✪ 1. Why do you think you are the best person for this job?
2. What do you want to happen next? What do you want from the person who receives your letter?

1 _____

2 _____

3 _____

4 _____

5 _____

What Do You Think?

✪ Why do you think Jamal wants to work as an engineer? Check (✓) the reasons.

☐ He doesn't like the workers at Crossroads Café.

☐ He wants to make more money.

☐ He does not think he is a good handyman.

☐ He went to school to learn engineering.

☐ He doesn't like to work for Mr. Brashov.

✪✪ Look at the sentences below. Check (✓) I agree, I disagree, or I don't know.

		I agree.	I disagree.	I don't know.
1.	Mr. Marshall, what you are doing is wrong!	☐	☐	☐
2.	I was the wrong person for the job.	☐	☐	☐
3.	Jamal, just do your job and sign the forms!	☐	☐	☐

✪✪✪ Answer the questions. Then read your sentences to someone.

1. Do you think what Mr. Marshall is doing is wrong? Tell why or why not.

_____

2. Do you think Jamal was the wrong person for the job? Tell why or why not.

_____

3. Do you think that Jamal should just do his job and sign the forms? Tell why or why not.

_____

Culture Clip: Worker Safety

⭐ Match.

1. There are laws about clothing and equipment to protect workers.

a.

2. There are laws to pay the expenses of injured workers.

b.

3. There is insurance to help workers who lose their jobs.

c.

⭐⭐ Complete the sentences. Write one in each blank. Use these words.

clothing	employers	expenses	wives
workers	jobs	social security	unemployment
worker's compensation			

Safety in the workplace is very important. It is a concern of government, workers, and _employers_. Some _____ are so dangerous that special _____ and safety
          (1)   (2)   (3)
equipment must be used to protect _____. Employers must have _____
                                        (4)   (5)
insurance to pay the _____ of employees who get hurt on the job. They also
                          (6)
have _____ insurance for workers who lose their jobs. _____ helps older
        (7)   (8)
workers and their husbands or _____ when they retire. Before accepting a new
                                  (9)
job, it is important to know if the employer has these employee programs.

⭐⭐⭐ Think.

Jamal doesn't think his new boss is concerned about safety rules. What would you do if you were Jamal? List some workplace safety rules that you know. What rules do you think are the most important? Why?

_____

_____

_____

Check Your English

⭐ Write the correct word under each picture.

happy people
cellular phone
hard hat
jukebox
angry person
computer

1.

2.

3.

happy people

4.

5.

6.

⭐⭐ Make a sentence or question from each group of words.

1. the   to   busier   Mr. Brashov   café   be   wants

   Mr. Brashov wants the café to be busier.

2. worried   safety   than   Mr. Marshall   is   Jamal   more   about

   _____

3. Jess   older   is   than   Jamal

   _____

4. thinks   rock   music   is   more   than   polka   music   is   Henry   popular

   _____

⭐⭐⭐ Finish the story. Use the words in the box. Write one word in each blank.

Mr. Brashov buys a jukebox for the café. He wants the customers to listen to

____music____ while they eat. One day a man named Mr. Marshall comes into the
   (1)

café. Mr. Marshall owns a construction _____. Mr. Marshall talks to Jamal
                                              (2)

about engineering and then offers him a _____. One night Jamal does some
                                              (3)

work with the _____. He finds that his new _____ uses _____
                   (4)   (5)   (6)

materials in his buildings. Jamal tells Mr. Marshall that the materials are not

_____. Mr. Marshall does not _____ to Jamal. Mr. Marshall offers
   (7)   (8)

_____ to Jamal. He wants Jamal to say that the _____ are O.K. Jamal
   (9)   (10)

says no to Mr. Marshall and then quits his _____ job. He then goes back
                                                (11)

to his _____ job.
          (12)

beams
boss
company
computer
engineering
handyman
job
jukebox
listen
materials
money
music
old
plug
safe

19 The People's Choice

In this unit you will:

- make promises
- read a water utility bill
- write a letter of complaint
- describe local government

Ways to Learn

Jess decides to **take a risk** and run for office as a city council member. He decides to **take a chance** and try something that seems impossible. To **take a risk** means to **take a chance**.

Take Risks

What is a **risk** for you? Fill in the blank with 1, 2, or 3.

1 = easy for me   **2 = a small risk**   **3 = a big risk**

___ start a conversation with a stranger
___ go to a meeting where people speak English
___ go to a party with English-speaking friends
___ ask for help from a coworker in English
___ write a letter to my landlord
___ call my child's teacher at school
___ invite an English-speaking friend for dinner
___ other: _____

On Your Own

When I **take a risk** with English, I feel afraid.	YES	NO
When I **take a risk** with English, I learn something.	YES	NO
I like to try English in **new situations**.	YES	NO

How will you **take a risk** next week?

1. I will _____

2. I will _____

Before You Watch

Look at the pictures. What do you see?

1.

2.

3.

4.

5.

6.

✪ What do you see in each picture? Write the number of the picture next to the word.

　_2_　election campaign 　　　　　_____　speech

　_____　reporters 　　　　　　　_____　water bill

　_____　newspaper article 　　　　_____　toupee

✪✪ What is happening? Write the number of the picture next to the sentence.

　_____　Jess is talking to the customers at the café.

　_1_　Mr. Brashov is looking at a water bill.

　_____　Reporters are listening to Jess's speech.

　_____　The Crossroads Café employees are putting letters in envelopes.

　_____　Jess has a toupee on his head.

　_____　Jess is showing Carol a newspaper article.

✪✪✪ Write one question you have about each picture. Then read your questions to someone.

1. Why does Mr. Brashov look upset? _____

2. _____

3. _____

4. _____

5. _____

6. _____

Focus For Watching　　Read the questions. Then watch.

✪ 1. Who has a problem with his water bill?
　2. Who wants to be a city councilman?

✪✪ 1. Who wants to build a downtown parking structure?
　2. Who will not vote for Jess?

✪✪✪ 1. Who doesn't understand why bad government officials are not replaced?
　2. Who is Jess's campaign manager?

After You Watch

What do you remember? Match each question with the correct picture. You can use a picture more than once.

⭐ 1. Who has a problem with his water bill?

a. Mr. Comstock

2. Who wants to be a city councilman?

b. Jess

⭐⭐ 1. Who wants to build a downtown parking structure?

c. Carol

2. Who will not vote for Jess?

d. Mr. Miller

⭐⭐⭐ 1. Who doesn't understand why bad government officials are not replaced?

2. Who is Jess's campaign manager?

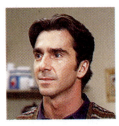

e. Hassan

✪ Read the sentences. Circle Yes or No.

1. Jess's water bill is $30,000.   (YES)   NO
2. The Crossroads Café employees want Jess to be city councilman.   YES   NO
3. Mr. Comstock gives Jess money for his campaign.   YES   NO
4. Jess wins the election.   YES   NO

✪✪ Put the sentences in order. Number 1 to 5.

_____   Jess loses the election.

_____   The Crossroads Café employees want Jess to run for office.

__1__   Jess is upset because his water bill is incorrect.

_____   Dan Miller and Andrew Comstock decide to support Jess.

_____   Carol is angry with Jess.

✪✪✪ Write the story. Use the five sentences above. Add these three sentences. Then close the book and tell the story to someone.

- She is unhappy because Jess supports the building of downtown parking structures.
- They want a candidate who will support business.
- The employees offer to help him with his campaign.

Jess is upset because his water bill is incorrect.

_____

_____

_____

_____

_____

_____

_____

_____

_____

_____

_____

_____

_____

Your New Language: Making Promises

I promise to work for the average citizen.

To tell someone that you will do something, you can say:

• I **promise to** work for the average citizen.

OR

• I **promise that I will** work for the average citizen.
• I **promise I will** work for the average citizen.

⭐ Complete the conversations. Use these phrases.

stop crime   cut taxes   support the average citizen
clean up

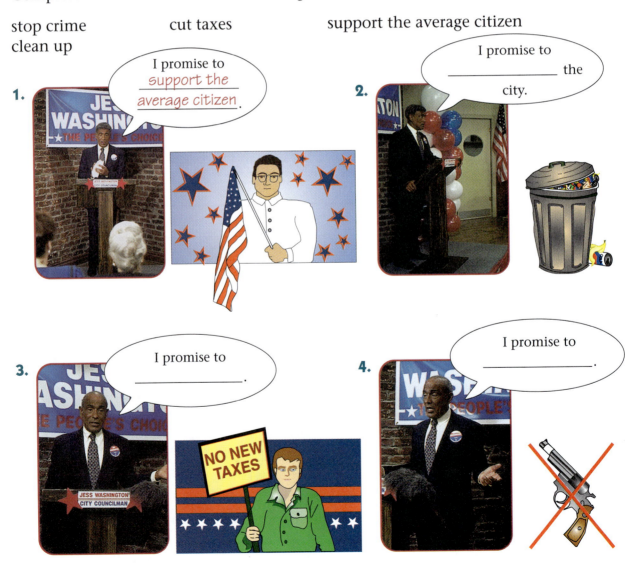

1. I promise to *support the average citizen*.

2. I promise to _____ the city.

3. I promise to _____.

4. I promise to _____.

✪✪ Match.

1. The city promised to repair the roads.
2. Politicians make too many promises.
3. I'll support you if you promise to help me build a parking structure.
4. What did she say about the bill?
5. Jess, I think you'll make a good city councilman.

a. Thank you. I promise I'll do my best.
b. I'm sorry. I can't promise to do that.
c. She promised to look into it.
d. I don't think there's enough money for roads.
e. I promise not to do that.

✪✪✪ Complete the conversation. Use these phrases. Write one phrase in each blank. You may use a phrase more than once.

promise to put
promise I will fight
promise to establish
promise to work

promised to cut
promise to repair
promise that the garbage will

REPORTER: Mr. Washington, if you are elected to the city council, what will you do?

JESS: Well, I __promise to work__ for the interests of the average citizen.
(1)

REPORTER: Does that mean you promise to create more jobs?

JESS: It sure does. It also means that I _____ the developers who want
(2)
to tear down the office buildings. I also _____ a hot line so
(3)
citizens can get answers to their questions. I _____ get collected
(4)
on a regular basis. I _____ more police officers on the street.
(5)
I _____ the roads. I promise I'll . . .
(6)

REPORTER: Mr. Washington, Mr. Washington, last year the city council _____
(7)
taxes. How can you make all these promises and cut taxes?

JESS: Uh. Good question.

★ Put the conversation in order. Number 1 to 3.

____ JESS: That's what I'm doing.

_1_ CAROL: You promised to work for the average citizen.

____ CAROL: No, Jess, you're not.

★★ Put the conversation in order. Number 1 to 4.

____ MR. COMSTOCK: I'm sure you will be. I'd like to offer my support. I believe in what you stand for.

____ JESS: Well, I hope they support me. I promise I'll be the best councilman.

____ JESS: Why, thank you. I promise to do a good job.

____ MR. COMSTOCK: Jess, I know a lot of people who are looking for a candiate to support.

★★★ Put the conversation in order. Number 1 to 6.

____ JESS: The same as my interests—safe neighborhoods, a clean city, good schools, and responsive government officials. These are the things I promise to work for.

____ JESS: I promise to work for the average citizen.

____ JESS: It means, I promise I'll listen to your concerns and work for your interests.

____ CITIZEN: Well that sounds good, but what does it mean?

____ CITIZEN: What will you do if you are elected to the city council?

____ CITIZEN: In your opinion, what are my interests?

In Your Community: Water Bills

This is the water bill Jess received. Answer the questions about the information on the bill. Then tell your answers to someone.

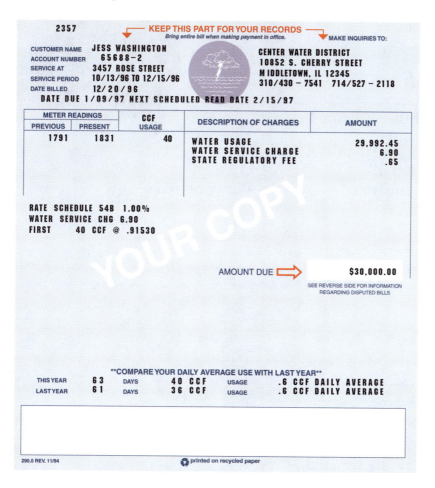

1. How much does Jess need to pay? _____

2. When must he pay the bill? _____

1. What is the service period of the bill? _____

2. If he has a question about the bill, what can he do? _____

_____

1. If Jess wants information about disputing this bill, what should he do? _____

_____

2. How does this year's usage compare to last year's? _____

_____

Now look at a water bill from your community. How is it the same as or different from this water bill?

Read and Write: Spotlight on Jess

Read the questions. Read Jess's letter very quickly to find the answers. Circle the answers.

 What does Jess write about?
a. a $300.00 water bill
b. a $30,000 water bill
c. a $3,000 water bill

⭐⭐ How does Jess feel about the situation?
a. surprised   b. angry   c. amused

⭐⭐⭐ What is the tone of this letter?
a. amused   b. frustrated   c. disappointed

Read the letter again carefully.

3457 Rose Street
Middletown, IL 12345

Center Water District
10852 Cherry Street
Middletown, IL 12345

To Whom It May Concern:
   I just got my water bill for $30,000! There is an error. I have attached a copy of my bill. I'm surprised your office didn't see the mistake. You can see that my daily usage is the same as last year's. I used the same amount of water every day last year that I used this year.
   I understand that I must pay this bill, even if I don't agree. Your office says that after I pay for it, I can dispute it. That's crazy.
   I don't have $30,000. I am retired and live on a pension.
   Please look at your records and investigate this as soon as possible.

Thank you.
Sincerely,

Jess Washington

Jess Washington

Find the word in the reading that means the same as the phrase below. Write the word next to the phrase.

⭐ **every day** _____

⭐⭐ **argue against** _____

⭐⭐⭐ **look carefully** _____

Now you write a letter of complaint to a utility (for example, gas, water, telephone, electricity) company. Give the following information.

⭐ Identify the problem

⭐⭐ Explain why you think there is a problem
Explain what you will or will not do

⭐⭐⭐ Request action

Read your letter to someone. Then ask: Did you understand?
Do you have questions?

What Do You Think?

⭐ Jess wants to be a city councilman. Check (✓) Yes, No, or I don't know.

	Yes.	No.	I don't know.
1. Do you think Jess should help the average citizen?	☐	☐	☐
2. Do you think Jess should help the business people?	☐	☐	☐

Which group is more important, average citizens or business people? Why do you think so?

⭐⭐ Look at the sentences below. Check (✓) I agree, I disagree, or I don't know.

	I agree.	I disagree.	I don't know.
1. If these city officials are not doing their jobs, they should be replaced.	☐	☐	☐
2. We don't want to tie the hands of our business community with unnecessary rules and regulations.	☐	☐	☐
3. I'll work for the interests of the people in the community.	☐	☐	☐

⭐⭐⭐ Answer the questions. Then read your answers to someone.

1. Do you think that city officials who don't do their jobs should be replaced? Tell why or why not.

_____

2. Do you think that business should be free of rules? Tell why or why not.

_____

3. Do you think that an elected official should work for the interests of its citizens? Tell why or why not.

_____

Culture Clip: Local Government

⭐ Match.

1. The mayor is the leader of the city.

2. The City Council makes the laws.

3. The judge and courts enforce the laws.

a.

b.

c.

⭐⭐ Complete the sentences. Write one word in each blank. Use these words.

govern	legislative	official	local
judicial	executive	trial	

There are three levels of ___local___ government. The mayor represents the
        (1)

_____ branch and is the _____ spokesperson for the city. The City
  (2)   (3)

Council represents the _____ branch. It makes the laws that _____
           (4)   (5)

the city. Judges represent the _____ branch. They handle both criminal
                  (6)

and civil cases that are brought to _____.
                        (7)

⭐⭐⭐ Jess decides to run for City Council because he is concerned about the average citizen. Do you think it's important for citizens to be active in their local governments? Why or why not? Write your ideas. Then tell your ideas to someone.

_____

_____

_____

_____

_____

Check Your English

✪ Write the correct word under each picture.

speech

newspaper
 article

election
 campaign

water bill

toupee

reporters

1.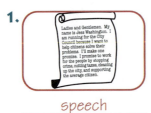

<u>speech</u>

2.

3.

4.

5.

6.

New Face on Local
Political Scene

✪✪ Make a sentence from each group of words.

1. to   help   I   the   average   promise   citizen

   <u>I promise to help the average citizen.</u>

2. city   cut   the   promised   to   taxes

   _____

3. I   that   I   promise   establish   a   will   hot   line

   _____

4. work   I   that   you   I   promise   for   will

   _____

✪✪✪ Finish the story. Use the words in the box. Write one word in each blank.

Jess receives a <u>water bill</u> for $30,000 in the mail. The bill is _____.
           (1)   (2)
He is so upset that the Crossroads Café employees suggest he _____ for
                                                            (3)
city council. His wife Carol thinks that this is a good idea because Jess would

represent the people well. Jess's _____ has a slow beginning. He makes
                                   (4)
_____ at Crossroads Café, but no one listens. One day two gentlemen
 (5)
come into the café. They think that if they _____ Jess he will help them
                                            (6)
develop the downtown area. Jess forgets that he is running to help the

_____ citizen. Carol gets very angry with Jess. She will not _____
  (7)   (8)
for him. Jess agrees with Carol. He _____ to work for the interests of the
                                     (9)
people in the community. On election night, Katherine calls election head-

quarters and gets the final number of _____. Jess has 18,422 votes, but that is not enough.
                                        (10)

average
businessmen
election
 campaign
incorrect
promise
promises
refund
run
speeches
support
vote
votes
water bill

20 Outside Looking In

In this unit you will:

- give advice
- read a movie guide
- write a letter about an uncomfortable situation
- identify cultural differences in raising children

Ways to Learn

Rosa wants to learn about art, music, and food. She can *take notes* to help remember what she reads and hears. *Taking notes* can help you remember English.

Take Notes

When I read I . . . (Check ✓)

- ☐ underline or circle important parts, then copy
- ☐ read headings, then write important words
- ☐ read the whole page and go back to write the important parts
- ☐ copy what I think I will forget
- ☐ other: _____

When I listen I . . . (Check ✓)

- ☐ write what I understand well
- ☐ write what I want to remember
- ☐ write questions
- ☐ write a summary
- ☐ other: _____

On Your Own

When did you *take notes* last week? _____

What problems do you have *taking notes* while reading?

- ☐ spelling
- ☐ finding word meanings
- ☐ understanding what I read

What problems do you have *taking notes* while listening?

- ☐ people talk too fast
- ☐ spelling
- ☐ deciding what to write
- ☐ knowing when to write

What will help you with these problems? _____

Before You Watch

Look at the pictures. What do you see?

1.

2.

3.

4.

5.

6.

⭐ What do you see in each picture? Write the number of the picture next to the word.

_6_ box   ____ vase

____ book   ____ graph

____ painting   ____ maid

⭐⭐ What is happening? Write the number of the picture next to the sentence.

_6_ Rosa is arguing with a man.

____ A man is showing people a graph.

____ Rosa is reading a book.

____ A maid is carrying a tray with food.

____ Several people are looking at a painting on the wall.

____ Rosa is looking at a very old vase.

⭐⭐⭐ Write one question you have about each picture. Then read your questions to someone.

1. Why is Rosa looking at the vase? _____

2. _____

3. _____

4. _____

5. _____

6. _____

Focus For Watching   Read the questions. Then watch.

⭐ 1. Who is Rosa's new teacher?
2. Who asks Rosa for help?

⭐⭐ 1. Who tries to learn more about art?
2. Who asks for Rosa's opinion about the painting?

⭐⭐⭐ 1. To whom does Rosa apologize?
2. Who tells Rosa that Andrew is too sophisticated for her?

After You Watch

What do you remember? Match each question with the correct picture. You can use a picture more than once.

a. Libby

⭐ 1. Who is Rosa's new teacher?

2. Who asks Rosa for help?

b. Rosa

⭐⭐ 1. Who tries to learn more about art?

2. Who asks for Rosa's opinion about the painting?

c. Andrew

⭐⭐⭐ 1. To whom does Rosa apologize?

d. the maid

2. Who tells Rosa that Andrew is too sophisticated for her?

★ Read the sentences. Circle Yes or No.
1. Rosa works for Andrew.   YES   (NO)
2. Libby likes Rosa.   YES   NO
3. Rosa learns more about art.   YES   NO
4. Andrew asks Rosa to go to Europe with him.   YES   NO

★★ Put the sentences in order. Number 1 to 4.

_____   Andrew and Rosa go out on a date.

_1_   Rosa's teacher, Andrew, comes to the café.

_____   Andrew gives Rosa a gift.

_____   Rosa goes to a party at Andrew's house.

★★★ Write the story. Use the four sentences above. Add these three sentences. Then close the book and tell the story to someone.
• Rosa is angry because Andrew is leaving for Europe.
• Andrew asks Rosa for help.
• She translates Spanish into English for the businesspeople.

Rosa's teacher, Andrew, comes to the café. Andrew asks Rosa for help.

_____

_____

_____

_____

_____

_____

_____

_____

_____

_____

_____

_____

_____

_____

Your New Language: Giving Advice

To give advice you can say:

- You **should** check to make sure.
- You **had better** check to make sure.

⭐ Complete the conversations. Use these phrases.

should try   get more experience   give me a raise   wear gloves

1.

2.

3.

4.

✪✪ Match.

1. I don't know what to do with Stuart.

2. I miss Andrew.

3. I'm really hungry.
4. Rosa works very hard.
5. I'd like you to meet Stuart.

a. You had better give her a raise.

b. You had better keep busy and forget about him.

c. You should bring him by to visit.
d. You should take him to a ball game.
e. You should try the special.

✪✪✪ Complete the conversation. Use these phrases. Write one in each blank.

should bring   had better think   should enroll   should go

MR. SHUSTER: I really don't know what to do with Stuart.

MR. BRASHOV: What do you mean?

MR. SHUSTER: He's ten years old, but acts like he's thirty.

KATHERINE: Maybe you ___should go___ camping or take him to a ball game. I
                              (1)
                         have a son. He likes to do those things.

MR. SHUSTER: Not Stuart. He likes to go to the library.

KATHERINE: Maybe you _____ him in a sports camp, like soccer.
                                              (2)

MR. SHUSTER: Hmm. I don't know.

MR. BRASHOV: You _____ him by to visit us. Maybe we can help you after
                              (3)
                         we meet him.

MR. SHUSTER: Thanks, maybe I'll do that. I need to think about this.

MR. BRASHOV: You _____ of something, because he's only ten once.
                              (4)

✪ Put the conversation in order. Number 1 to 3.

__1__ ROSA: You should try our special, Chicken Molé.

_____ JESS: Too bad. Rosa's specials are wonderful. You really should try it.

_____ ANDREW: Thanks, Rosa, but I'm not hungry.

✪✪ Put the conversation in order. Number 1 to 5.

_____ ROSA: Thanks, Jamal. Those are great ideas.

_____ ROSA: I want to talk about art with Andrew.

_____ JAMAL: You should also visit some museums.

_____ ROSA: That's what I'm planning to do.

_____ JAMAL: You should get some books from the library.

✪✪✪ Put the conversation in order. Number 1 to 6.

_____ KATHERINE: I think you should keep busy. Let's go to the movies this weekend.

_____ KATHERINE: You had better stop that. You know he's not interested in you.

_____ ROSA: I don't know. I guess I miss Andrew.

_____ KATHERINE: Rosa, what's the matter with you?

_____ ROSA: I know that. What do you think I should do?

_____ ROSA: Thanks for the advice and the invitation, Katherine.

In Your Community: Movie Guide

This is the movie guide Katherine looked at in the newspaper. Answer the questions. Then tell your answers to someone.

MOVIE GUIDE

Movie Review

Elizabeth's Wedding- A comedy about a young woman who wants to get married, but always finds the wrong guy. (PG-13)

Nowhere to be Found- An action-packed movie about a man looking for his missing wife. (R) **

Baby- A children's story about a mother bear and her young cubs. (G)

In the Darkness- An extremely violent movie about one police officer's fight against crime in the big city. (NC-17)**

NOW PLAYING

Central City
Center Plaza Cinemas
(217) 555-4444

Nowhere to be Found
12:15, 2:45, 5:15, 7:30, 9:45
Baby
11:00, 12:30, 2:30, 4:00, 5:30
Home Again
12:45, 4:45, 7:15, 9:00, 10:15

New Park
Park Movie House
(217) 555-0089

Elizabeth's Wedding
1:00, 2:45, 4:45,
6:15, 8:00, 10:15
Nowhere to be Found
12:30, 3:00, 5:30, 7:45, 9:15

Brenthill
Brenthill Cinemas
(217) 555-0987

In the Darkness
12:15, 2:45, 5:15, 7:30, 9:45
Nowhere to be Found
12:00, 2:45, 5:15, 7:00, 9:15

Movie categories:
(G) for general audiences; (PG) parental guidance; (PG-13) children under 13 should not attend; (R) restricted, younger than 17 only with parents, (NC-17) no one younger than 17 admitted. Movies considered excellent by our movie critic are marked with a **

⭐ 1. Where is *Elizabeth's Wedding* playing? _____

2. At what times is *Baby* playing? _____

⭐⭐ 1. What two movies show at the same times? _____

2. What does ** mean? _____

⭐⭐⭐ What movies require that children go with their parents? _____

_____

_____

Find the movie listing in your newspaper. How is it the same as or different from this listing?

Read and Write: Spotlight on Rosa

This is a letter that Rosa wrote to a friend of hers.
Read the questions. Read Rosa's letter very
quickly to find the answers. Circle the answers.

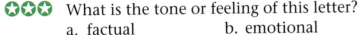

⭐ What does Rosa write about?
   a. her busy schedule
   b. a man she liked
   c. a trip to Switzerland

⭐⭐ How does she feel about what she did?
   a. angry   b. sad   c. embarassed

⭐⭐⭐ What is the tone or feeling of this letter?
   a. factual   b. emotional   c. apologetic

Read the letter again carefully.

Dear Carmen,

   It was nice to get your letter. I'm glad that all is well with you. I'm sorry
that I didn't write sooner, but I was really busy.

   I met a man that I really liked. He asked me to help him translate for some
South American businesspeople. We went on a few dates. I was interested in
him. I thought that he was interested in me, too. I was naive to think
that. He moved to Switzerland last week. At first I was hurt that he was
leaving. Then I got angry. I am too embarassed to tell you what I did. It
wasn't very nice. I am going to write Andrew a letter of apology. I hope that
he will forgive me and that we can be friends. He is really a nice guy, but not
my type!

   I hope that all is well with you. Give my love to your family.

Love, Rosa

Find the word in the reading. What does it mean? Circle the answer.

⭐ **hurt:**
   a. feel angry   b. feel badly   c. feel happy

⭐⭐ **forgive:**
   a. apologize   b. accept an apology   c. not remember

⭐⭐⭐ **naive:**
   a. suspicious   b. childlike   c. hopeful

Now you write a letter about something you did that you are not happy about. In your letter answer the following questions.

⭐ What did you do?
How do you feel?

⭐⭐ Why did you do it?

⭐⭐⭐ What are you going to do to make things better?

Dear   ,

_____

_____

_____

_____

_____

_____

_____

_____

_____

_____

_____

_____

_____

_____

_____

_____

_____

Love,

_____

Read your entry to someone. Then ask: Did you understand?
Do you have questions?

What Do You Think?

⭐ Who do you think was the most honest about themselves? Circle the name.

Andrew

Libby

Rosa

⭐⭐ Look at the sentences below. Check (✓) I agree, I disagree, or I don't know.

	I agree.	I disagree.	I don't know.

1.

I hope you won't take this the wrong way, Rosa, but you are out of your league. Andrew is too sophisticated for you.

☐   ☐   ☐

2.

I was naive. I thought there was more going on between Andrew and me than there really was.

☐   ☐   ☐

⭐⭐⭐ Answer the questions. Then read your answers to someone.

1. Do you think people should pretend to be something they are not? Tell why or why not.

_____

_____

2. Do you think people can change who they are? Tell why or why not.

_____

_____

Culture Clip: Raising Children

⭐ Match.

1. Children sometimes do not respect their parents.

a.

2. Having children is important in many cultures.

b.

3. Parents sometimes buy their children too many things.

c.

⭐⭐ Complete the sentences. Write one word in each blank. Use these words.

respect	raised	television	goods
expected	culture	worry	challenging

In many cultures married couples are __expected__ to have children. Having a
                                        (1)
family is very important. How children are _____ is often determined by
                                              (2)
the parents' _____. Newcomers to the United States often _____
               (3)   (4)
about raising their children here. They worry about the lack of _____ for
                                                                    (5)
elders, the emphasis on material _____, and the amount of _____
                                    (6)   (7)
children watch. For immigrant parents, raising children in a new country is

_____.
   (8)

⭐⭐⭐ Mr. Brashov's landlord, Mr. Shuster, is worried about how he is raising his
son. Do you think it's difficult to raise children? Why or why not? Write
your ideas. Then tell your ideas to someone.

_____

_____

_____

_____

Check Your English

✪ Write the correct word under each picture.

book

maid

vase

graph

box

painting

1.

book

2.

_____

3.

_____

4.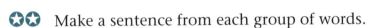

_____

5.

_____

6.

_____

✪✪ Make a sentence from each group of words.

1. you   him   to   should   take   movies   the

You should take him to the movies.

2. class   you   a   about   take   modern   should   art

_____

3. bring   you   him   should   to   visit   by

_____

4. had   you   very   keep   busy   better

_____

✪✪✪ Finish the story. Use the words in the box. Write one word in each blank.

Andrew Collins, Rosa's teacher, comes to Crossroads Café to ask Rosa for
help. He does not speak Spanish. He needs Rosa to __translate__ from Spanish
                                                        (1)
to English for some South American businesspeople. Rosa agrees to help and
goes to a party at his apartment. There are many _____ guests,
                                                      (2)
including Andrew's friend, Libby. Rosa is not _____. However, she is so
                                                   (3)
_____ with Andrew that she begins to study _____ and fine
   (4)   (5)
_____. Rosa likes Andrew and she thinks he likes her. They go on
   (6)
several _____. One day Andrew asks Rosa to come to his apartment.
            (7)
When she arrives, Andrew tells her that he is _____ to Europe. Andrew
                                                   (8)
gives Rosa a gift to show his _____ for her help. Rosa is angry and hurt.
                                  (9)
She returns the gift and leaves the apartment immediately.

appreciation
art
buffet
comfortable
dates
impressed
interested
moving
paintings
sophisticated
translate
vases
wines

21 Walls and Bridges

In this unit you will:

- ask for and offer help
- read a report card
- write a note
- identify steps in becoming a citizen

Ways to Learn

Mr. Brashov studies for American citizenship. His friends help him study to pass the test. Everyone learns by *teaching others*. One way to learn English is to *teach others* what you know.

Teach Others

Check (✓) ways you *teach others*.

- ☐ I explain the meaning of words to friends and family.
- ☐ I tell a classmate about grammar rules.
- ☐ I read to my children in English.
- ☐ I summarize lessons for my teacher or friends.
- ☐ I write new words or sentences for friends or family.
- ☐ I show a coworker how to do a job.
- ☐ I make tapes of new words or phrases for friends.
- ☐ other: _____

On Your Own

Teaching others what I learned helps me remember new words and phrases.   YES   NO

Teaching others is difficult for me.   YES   NO

Tell how you will *teach others* next week.

Who	What I will teach
_____	_____
_____	_____
_____	_____

Before You Watch

Look at the pictures. What do you see?

1.

2.

3.

4.

5.

6.

✪ What do you see in each picture? Write the number of the picture next to the word.

_6_ citizenship book   ____ tailor shop

____ lunch box   ____ skirt

____ proud people   ____ teary eyes

✪✪ What is happening? Write the number of the picture next to the sentence.

_6_ Mr. Brashov studies for the citizenship test.

____ A tailor shortens Rosa's skirt.

____ A girl hands a man a lunch box.

____ Rosa and another woman go to the tailor.

____ The girl shows Rosa a photograph.

____ The girl is sad.

✪✪✪ Write one question you have about each picture. Then read your questions to someone.

1. What is the job of the man with the broom? _____

2. _____

3. _____

4. _____

5. _____

6. _____

Focus For Watching   Read the questions. Then watch.

✪ 1. Who has two jobs?
   2. Who stays home from school to work?
   3. Who comes to the café to talk to Rosa about María?

✪✪ 1. Who says María is an honor student?
   2. Who talks to María's parents about school?
   3. Who writes a goodbye letter?

✪✪✪ 1. Who first suggests a work-study program?
   2. Who arranges for a work-study program?
   3. Who talks with Mr. Hernandez about giving María a chance?

After You Watch

What do you remember? Match each question with the correct picture. You can use a picture more than once.

⭐ 1. Who has two jobs?

a. María Hernandez

2. Who stays home from school to work?

3. Who comes to the café to talk to Rosa about María?

b. César Hernandez

⭐⭐ 1. Who says María is an honor student?

c. Rosa

2. Who talks to María's parents about school?

3. Who writes a good-bye letter?

d. Chris Scanlon

⭐⭐⭐ 1. Who first suggests a work-study program?

e. Henry

2. Who arranges for the work-study program?

3. Who talks with Mr. Hernandez about giving María a chance?

f. Mr. Brashov

✪ Read the sentences. Circle Yes or No.
1. María has to work for her family.   (YES)   NO
2. María is not a very good student.   YES   NO
3. María can go to school and work.   YES   NO

✪✪ Put the sentences in order. Number 1 to 4.

_____   Mrs. Scanlon arranges a work-study program for María.

_____   Mr. Brashov convinces Mr. Hernandez that María should go to school.

_1_   Mrs. Scanlon asks Rosa to talk to María's parents.

_____   Rosa discovers María is helping out in her father's shop.

✪✪✪ Write the story. Use the four sentences above. Add these three sentences. Then close the book and tell the story to someone.
• Mrs. Scanlon tells Rosa that María hasn't been going to school.
• Mrs. Scanlon arranges for a worker in the retraining program to work in Mr. Hernandez's shop.
• María gives Rosa a letter for Mrs. Scanlon.

Mrs. Scanlon tells Rosa that María hasn't been going to school. Mrs. Scanlon asks Rosa

to talk to María's parents.

_____

_____

_____

_____

_____

_____

_____

_____

_____

_____

_____

Your New Language: Asking for and Offering Help

Unfortunately, I don't speak Spanish. Would you talk to them for me?

To ask for help, you can say:

- **Please** _____ for me.
  - talk to them
  - fix it

- **Would** you _____ for me?
  - talk to them
  - fix it

To offer to help, you can say

- **I'd be glad to** _____.
  - talk to them
  - fix it

★ Complete the conversations. Use these phrases.

give her this letter   talk to them   shorten it   arrange one

1.

Mrs. Scanlon asked me about you.

Please
give her this letter
for me.

2.

Did you talk to María's parents?

No. Would you _____ for me?

3.

Did Henry suggest a work-study program for María?

Yes. Would you _____ for her?

4.

This skirt needs to be shorter.

I'd be glad to _____.

✪✪ Match.

1. I've lost my keys again.
2. Would you like me to help you study for the test?
3. I can't understand this. Would you explain it to me?
4. Would you help me lift this? It's heavy.
5. Please photocopy this for me.

a. Sure. I'd be happy to explain it.
b. I don't know how to use the photocopier. Would you show me?
c. I'm sorry, but I can't. I have a bad back.
d. Thank you, but I don't need any help studying.
e. Would you like me to help you look for them?

✪✪✪ Complete the conversation. Use these words. Write one word in each blank. You may use a word more than once.

Would you   I'd be glad to   Please   Please help me

MARÍA: <u>Would you</u> deliver this letter to Mrs. Scanlon for me?
         (1)

ROSA: What is it? A good-bye letter?

MARÍA: Yes. I can't go to school any more. My father needs my help in the shop.

ROSA: María, you can work and go to school.

MARÍA: I can do that? How?

ROSA: Mrs. Scanlon can arrange for a work-study program.

MARÍA: _____ talk to her for me.
         (2)

ROSA: _____.
         (3)

MARÍA: I'm afraid my father won't like the idea. _____ convince him.
                                                        (4)

ROSA: _____ help convince him.
         (5)

⭐ Put the conversation in order. Number 1 to 3.

_____ KATHERINE: What?

_____ ROSA: Please explain this word.

__1__ ROSA: Would you do me a favor?

⭐⭐ Put the conversation in order. Number 1 to 4.

_____ KATHERINE: This box is heavy. Would you help me lift it?

_____ HENRY: What's wrong?

_____ KATHERINE: Thanks a lot.

_____ HENRY: Sure. I'd be glad to lend you a hand.

⭐⭐⭐ Put the conversation in order. Number 1 to 5.

_____ MRS. SCANLON: I don't speak Spanish. Would you translate this note for me?

_____ MRS. SCANLON: Thanks anyway.

_____ ROSA: What can I do?

_____ ROSA: I'm afraid I don't have time right now.

_____ MRS. SCANLON: I need your help.

In Your Community: Report Cards

This is a copy of María's report card. Answer the questions about the card. Then share your answers with someone.

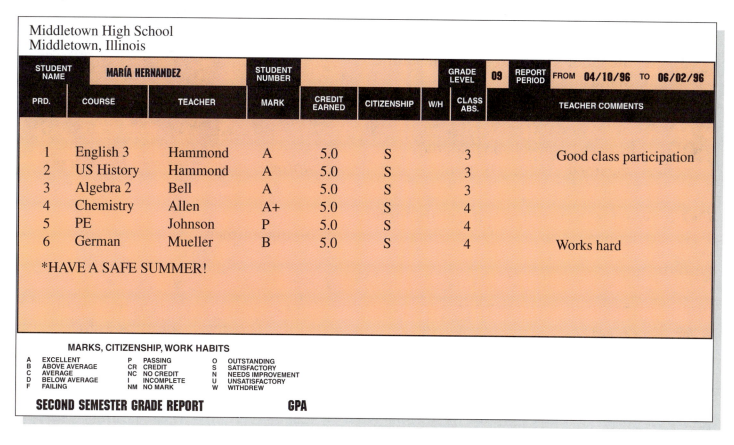

Middletown High School
Middletown, Illinois

| STUDENT NAME | MARÍA HERNANDEZ | | STUDENT NUMBER | | | GRADE LEVEL | 09 | REPORT PERIOD | FROM 04/10/96 TO 06/02/96 |

PRD.	COURSE	TEACHER	MARK	CREDIT EARNED	CITIZENSHIP	W/H	CLASS ABS.	TEACHER COMMENTS
1	English 3	Hammond	A	5.0	S		3	Good class participation
2	US History	Hammond	A	5.0	S		3	
3	Algebra 2	Bell	A	5.0	S		3	
4	Chemistry	Allen	A+	5.0	S		4	
5	PE	Johnson	P	5.0	S		4	
6	German	Mueller	B	5.0	S		4	Works hard

*HAVE A SAFE SUMMER!

MARKS, CITIZENSHIP, WORK HABITS

A	EXCELLENT	P	PASSING	O	OUTSTANDING
B	ABOVE AVERAGE	CR	CREDIT	S	SATISFACTORY
C	AVERAGE	NC	NO CREDIT	N	NEEDS IMPROVEMENT
D	BELOW AVERAGE	I	INCOMPLETE	U	UNSATISFACTORY
F	FAILING	NM	NO MARK	W	WITHDREW

SECOND SEMESTER GRADE REPORT   **GPA**

⭐ 1. How many classes is María taking? _____

2. What does María's English teacher say about her? _____

⭐⭐ 1. Which class gives a pass/fail rather than a letter grade? _____

2. Which class is most difficult for María? _____

⭐⭐⭐ 1. Why do you think María got an A+ in the chemistry class? _____

_____

2. Why would María have a different number of absences for periods 1, 2, and 3 than for periods 4, 5, and 6? _____

3. If María were your daughter, how would you feel about her report card?

_____

Now look at the report card of someone you know. How is it the same as or different from María's report card?

Read and Write: Spotlight on Rosa

Read the questions. Read Rosa's note very quickly to find the answers. Circle the answers.

⭐ What does Rosa write about?
  a. the tailor shop and sewing machine
  b. María and school
  c. Crossroads Café and customers

⭐⭐ How does Rosa feel about María?
  a. ashamed   b. proud   c. worried

⭐⭐⭐ What is the tone or feeling of this note?
  a. appreciation   b. boredom   c. disappointment

Read the note again carefully.

Mr. Hernandez,

Thank you for meeting with Mrs. Scanlon and me yesterday. You and your wife have a wonderful daughter.

As you know, María is an honor student. Mrs. Scanlon says María can get a scholarship for college. If she continues to get good grades, there may be enough money to pay for all her college expenses! We are both very proud of María.

It is fun to be María's big sister. I am glad the school has a program for people in the community to help students. I enjoy the Big Sister Program because María is my "little" sister.

Rosa

Find the words in the reading that mean the same as the phrases below. Write the words below the phrases.

⭐ a person who gets good grades

_____

⭐⭐ money to pay for college expenses

_____

⭐⭐⭐ a program for people in the community to help students

_____

Now you write a thank-you note to someone for meeting with you.

⭐ Write the person's name.
Thank the person for the meeting.
Say when the meeting was.
Say what the meeting was about.
Sign your name.

✪✪ Add another paragraph:
Summarize what you talked about in the meeting.
Tell how you feel about the meeting.

✪✪✪ Add one more paragraph:
Give some new information related to the subject of the meeting, but not discussed in the meeting.

Read your note to someone. Then ask: Did you understand?
Do you have questions?

What Do You Think?

✪ What should María do? Check (✓) one.
- ☐ She should quit school and help her father.
- ☐ She should stay in school full-time.
- ☐ She should go to school part-time and help her father part-time.

✪✪ Look at the sentences below. Check (✓) I agree, I disagree, or I don't know.

		I agree.	I disagree.	I don't know.
1.	I owe this country a lot.	☐	☐	☐
2.	It is difficult to accept help.	☐	☐	☐
3.	María will marry and have childen. She doesn't need to go to college for that.	☐	☐	☐

✪✪✪ Answer the questions. Then read your answers to someone.

1. Do you owe this country a lot? Tell why or why not.

_____

_____

2. Is it difficult for you to accept help? Tell why or why not.

_____

_____

3. Should women who plan to marry and have children go to college? Tell why or why not.

_____

_____

Culture Clip: Becoming a Citizen

✪ Match.

1. Nancy wants to be a citizen because of her family.

a.

2. She gets help from a counselor at the adult school.

b.

3. Finally, she becomes a citizen.

c.

✪✪ Complete the sentences. Write one word in each blank. Use these words.

application	exam	government	citizen
English	interview	citizenship	fingerprints
procedure			

When Nancy decided to become a citizen, she went to a school outreach center. A counselor explained the _procedure_ to become a citizen. Nancy attended _____
(1)   (2)
classes at the school. The school helped her get _____ and photos for the _____
(3)   (4)
packet. Nancy studied for the _____ while she waited for the INS to respond to her
(5)
application. At her _____, she answered questions about United States _____
(6)   (7)
and history, as well as questions about herself. She also had to write a sentence in
_____. Finally, she was sworn in and became a naturalized U.S. _____.
(8)   (9)

✪✪✪ Nancy says, "It was hard to give up my Guatamalen citizenship because I was afraid I was betraying my country." Does becoming a U.S. citizen mean giving up your traditions and customs? Write your ideas. Then tell your ideas to someone.

_____

_____

_____

Check Your English

⭐ Write the correct word under each picture.

citizenship
  book

skirt

proud people

lunch box

teary eyes

tailor shop

1.
citizenship book

2.
_____

3.
_____

4.
_____

5.
_____

6. _____

★★ Make a sentence or question from each group of words.

1. close   please   help   this   me   suitcase

   Please help me close this suitcase. _____

2. homework   María   her   help   do   please

  _____

3. glad   machine   you   that   I'd   for   fix   be   to

  _____

4. would   me   this   word   you   define   for

  _____

★★★ Finish the story. Use the words in the box. Write one word in each blank.

Rosa is a "big sister" to María Hernandez, a high school student.

An <u>honor student</u>, María has a good chance of getting scholarships to
      (1)

_____, but she hasn't been in school for several weeks. Mrs. Scanlon
(2)

doesn't speak _____, so she asks Rosa to talk to María's parents. When
        (3)

Rosa goes to the Hernandez _____ shop, she discovers María is
              (4)

_____ in the shop. The next day María tells Rosa that her father had
(5)

to _____ a seamstress. She gives Rosa a good-bye letter for Mrs. Scanlon.
  (6)

When Rosa suggests that María deliver the letter herself, María starts to

_____. Mrs. Scanlon arranges for María to go to _____ and for
(7)   (8)

the shop to have a part-time worker while María is in school.

café
college
cry
English
high school
hire
honor
  student
laugh
lay off
school
Spanish
tailor
working

22 Helping Hands

In this unit you will:

- ask for and give permission
- read a résumé
- write a letter of complaint
- identify solutions to money problems

Ways to Learn

The employees at Crossroads Café try to help Frank get ready for a job interview. They all learn that *practicing* is an important way to prepare for an interview. One way to learn English is to *practice often*.

Practice Often

Check (✓) ways you *practice* English at home, at work, or in the community.

- ☐ I repeat words or phrases several times.
- ☐ I listen to English tapes or radio and TV programs.
- ☐ I write words, sentences, and paragraphs in English.
- ☐ I write in a journal.
- ☐ I write notes to English-speaking friends.
- ☐ I keep a notebook of grammar rules and write sentences using the rules.
- ☐ other: _____

On Your Own

When and how did you *practice* English last week?

When	How
_____	_____
_____	_____
_____	_____
_____	_____

Before You Watch

Look at the pictures. What do you see?

1.

2.

3.

4.

5.

6.

✪ What do you see in each picture? Write the number of the picture next to the word.

<u> 3 </u>   flashlight   <u>   </u>   crib

<u>   </u>   bench   <u>   </u>   baby

<u>   </u>   typewriter   <u>   </u>   pockets

✪✪ What is happening? Write the number of the picture next to the sentence.

<u> 6 </u>   Jamal is unhappy with Jihan.

<u>   </u>   Jess holds a flashlight for Mr. Brashov.

<u>   </u>   A man sits on a bench outside the café.

<u>   </u>   Henry types something for the man.

<u>   </u>   Jamal enters the hotel room with his baby.

<u>   </u>   The man has his hands in the pockets of his coat.

✪✪✪ Write one question you have about each picture. Then read your questions to someone.

1. <u>Who is the man outside the café?</u>

2. _____

3. _____

4. _____

5. _____

6. _____

Focus For Watching   Read the questions. Then watch.

✪ 1. Who is the man on the bench?
   2. Who goes on a trip?

✪✪ 1. Who loses his luggage?
    2. Who needs to hire an auto mechanic?

✪✪✪ 1. Who helps Mr. Brashov fix the lights in the café?
     2. Who helps the man relax for his job interview?

After You Watch

What do you remember? Match each question with the correct picture. You can use a picture more than once.

⭐ 1. Who is the man
   on the bench?

a. Frank

2. Who goes on a trip?

b. Jamal

⭐⭐ 1. Who loses his luggage?

2. Who needs to hire an
   auto mechanic?

c. Marty

⭐⭐⭐ 1. Who helps Mr. Brashov
   fix the lights in the café?

d. Katherine

2. Who helps the man relax
   for his job interview?

✪ Read the sentence. Circle Yes or No.

1. Frank is a businessperson.   YES   (NO)
2. Jamal has a good time on his trip.   YES   NO
3. Marty interviews Frank for a job.   YES   NO
4. Frank does excellent work at the café.   YES   NO

✪✪ Put the sentences in order. Number 1 to 4.

_____ Mr. Brashov helps Frank by giving him some handyman work while Jamal is on vacation.

_____ After his second interview, Frank is offered a job as a mechanic.

__1__ One day, an unemployed man named Frank comes into the café.

_____ Frank does excellent work as a handyman, so everyone works together to help him get a new job.

✪✪✪ Write the story. Use the four sentences above. Add these four sentences. Then close the book and tell the story to someone.

• Everyone thinks that Frank is trying to rob the café, so they put up their hands.
• He is hungry and asks for something to eat.
• Frank does not do well in his first job interview, but he gets another chance.
• After awhile everyone realizes that Frank is not a criminal, but someone who really wants to work.

One day, an unemployed man named Frank comes into the café. He is hungry and asks for

something to eat.

_____

_____

_____

_____

_____

_____

_____

_____

_____

_____

_____

Your New Language: Asking for and Giving Permission

(speech bubble) May I take a look at the box?

To ask for permission you can say:

- **May I** take a look?
- **Can I** take a look?
- **Do you mind if I** take a look?

- **May I** use your pen?
- **Can I** use your pen?
- **Do you mind if I** use your pen?

★ Complete the conversations. Use these words.

go   take   leave   have

1.

(speech bubble) What's the matter, Katherine?

(speech bubble) My daughter is sick. May I _____leave_____ now to pick her up at school?

2.

(speech bubble) May I _____ a look at the electrical box?

(speech bubble) Sure, go ahead. I hope you can find out what is wrong.

(speech bubble) Oh great! The fan over the stove isn't working.

3.

(speech bubble) Why are you still here, Mr. Washington? Is there a problem with your car?

(speech bubble) Yes, it didn't start today. May I _____ a ride to the bus station?

4.

(speech bubble) What's the problem? Can I _____ into the kitchen to see what's wrong with it?

✪✪ Match.

1. Do you mind if I watch the news?

2. May I borrow your book?

3. Do you mind if I smoke?

4. May I take tomorrow off from work?

a. I'm sorry, but this is a smoke-free restaurant.

b. No, I don't think so. We'll need you here because we're going to be very busy.

c. Sure. I think you'll really like the story.

d. No, go ahead. The TV won't bother me at all.

✪✪✪ Complete the conversation. Use these phrases. Write one phrase in each blank. You may use a phrase more than once.

may I   do you mind   can I

JESS: Oh, great. My car won't start.

FRANK: What's the matter with it? __Do you mind__ if I take a look?
                                        (1)

JESS: Not at all. Maybe there's a problem with the battery since it's so cold out there.

FRANK: Maybe, but let's be sure. _____ have your car keys for a minute?
                                         (2)

JESS: Sure. Here they are. _____ help you do anything?
                                    (3)

FRANK: No, not right now. I'll go out and see if I can find the problem. I'll be right back.

JESS: _____ if I watch you while you're working? I might learn something
              (4)
          new about this old car of mine.

FRANK: Sure. Let's hope we can find the problem quickly. If we can't, _____
                                                                              (5)
          if I work on it tomorrow? It will be warmer then.

✪ Put the conversation in order. Number 1 to 4.

____	MR. BRASHOV:	I guess it's O.K. We're not that busy.
1	KATHERINE:	Mr. Brashov, may I leave a little early today?
____	MR. BRASHOV:	Why don't you leave now? Call me later to let me know how she is.
____	KATHERINE:	Thanks. My daughter is sick and I'm taking her to the doctor.

✪✪ Put the conversation in order. Number 1 to 5.

____	CUSTOMER:	Do you mind if I smoke?
____	KATHERINE:	No, no problem. I'll take your drink over for you.
____	KATHERINE:	I'm sorry, but smoking is not allowed in this section of the restaurant.
____	CUSTOMER:	Do you mind if I move to another table?
____	CUSTOMER:	Thanks.

✪✪✪ Put the conversation in order. Number 1 to 6.

____	JAMAL:	No. This is all I have. Is there something else that could help?
____	FRANK:	Can I give you a hand with that pipe?
____	JAMAL:	No. I don't mind. I'll use anything that can help me get this pipe back into the sink.
____	JAMAL:	Sure. Can you hand me the wrench?
____	FRANK:	Sure. Here you go. Don't you have a special wrench for this kind of pipe?
____	FRANK:	Yes. Do you mind if we use my wrench instead of this one?

In Your Community: Résumés

Read Frank's résumé. Answer the questions about the résumé. Then tell your answers to someone.

FRANK B. NUSSMAN
124 Maplewood Avenue, # 245
Middletown, IL 12345
Phone: (217) 555-3728

PROFESSIONAL EXPERIENCE

Factory Worker, G & R Automobile Manufacturing
Company, Middletown, Illinois (6 months)
- Worked on automobile assembly line
- Prepared automobiles for delivery

Auto Mechanic, Highbridge Auto Center, Middletown,
Illinois (3 years)
- Worked on tires, brakes, oil filters, mufflers and
  wheels on domestic cars, trucks and vans
- Conducted state car inspections
- Designed a computerized customer billing system

Auto Center Manager/Tow Truck Operator,
Neighborhood Service Center, Chicago, Illinois
(15 years)
- Repaired both foreign and domestic cars
- Coordinated 24-hour emergency towing service
- Supervised staff of ten auto mechanics

EDUCATION

High School Equivalency (G.E.D.) Diploma,
Charleton Adult Learning Center, Chicago, Illinois

REFERENCES
Available upon request

⭐ 1. How long did Frank work in a factory? _____

2. What three kinds of vehicles can Frank repair? _____

3. What towns has Frank worked in? _____

⭐⭐ 1. Where did Frank work the longest? _____

2. Did Frank ever drive vehicles as part of his job? Tell how you know.

_____

3. Does Frank have any experience with computers? Tell how you know.

_____

⭐⭐⭐ 1. Marty asks Frank if he has any supervisory experience. What would Frank say?

_____

2. You have a problem with the air conditioning system in your foreign car. Could
Frank repair it for you? Tell why or why not.

_____

Look at two résumés. How are they the same as or different from Frank's? Tell your
answers to someone.

Read and Write: Spotlight on Jamal

Jamal writes a letter to the airline to complain. Read the letter very quickly to find the answers. Circle the answers.

⭐ What does Jamal write about?
a. his work   b. his vacation   c. a missing bag

⭐⭐ How does Jamal feel about the airline?
a. satisfied   b. angry   c. nervous

⭐⭐⭐ What is the tone or feeling of this letter?
a. friendly   b. hopeful   c. serious

Read the letter again carefully.

Mr. Ralph Madison
South Airlines
1540 West 101st Street-Suite 3100
Chicago, Illinois 60613

Dear Mr. Madison:

   I am writing this letter to tell you about a problem I have with your airline. My daughter and I took a trip on Flight #345 on April 15. As I write this, I am still missing one large piece of luggage.

   When we arrived at our destination, I asked about my luggage. They told me they would find it. They found two bags, but one is still missing.

   The bag contains my camera, my wife's paperwork and most of my clothes. As a result of your mistake, we couldn't take any pictures on our vacation. My wife was not well prepared for her business meetings, and I had to purchase new clothes.

   You must agree that this has been a rather costly mistake. I would appreciate it if you would look into this matter as soon as possible. I will never do business with your airline again unless this matter is resolved to my satisfaction.

Sincerely yours,

Jamal Al-Jibali

Jamal Al-Jibali

Find the words in the reading. What do they mean? Circle the answer.

⭐ To **purchase** means:
a. to wear
b. to look
c. to buy

⭐⭐ **Destination** means:
a. a place someone leaves from
b. a place someone goes
c. a place someone lives

⭐⭐⭐ To **resolve** means:
a. to find something that is missing
b. to find an answer to a problem
c. to start an argument

Now you write a letter complaining about something. Make sure your letter looks like Jamal's. In your letter, include the following information.

⭐ 1. the name of the person you are writing to
   2. the address of the person
   3. what the problem is
   4. your signature
   5. a closing (sincerely, yours truly, etc.)

⭐⭐ 1. how this problem has made things difficult for you
    2. how you want the problem solved

⭐⭐⭐ 1. what you plan to do if the problem is not solved

Read your letter to someone. Then ask: Did you understand?
Do you have questions?

What Do You Think?

⭐ Why is Jamal angry with Jihan? Check (✓) the reasons.

☐ He doesn't like to go on vacation.

☐ Jihan doesn't spend much time with him.

☐ Jihan makes a lot more money than he does.

☐ Jihan does not help him with the baby.

☐ Jihan works a lot of hours.

⭐⭐ Look at the sentences below. Check (✓) I agree, I disagree, or I don't know.

	I agree.	I disagree.	I don't know.
1. Frank could help himself if he really wanted to.	☐	☐	☐
2. You think your job is more important than your family.	☐	☐	☐
3. You want me to quit my job and stay home.	☐	☐	☐

⭐⭐⭐ Answer the questions. Then read your answers to someone.

1. Do you think Frank could help himself if he really wanted to? Tell why or why not.

_____

2. Do you think that a job is more important than a family? Tell why or why not.

_____

3. Do you think Jihan should quit her job and stay home? Tell why or why not.

_____

Culture Clip: Financial Difficulties

✪ Match.

1. Not having enough money causes problems.

a.

2. One problem is children grow up too quickly.

b.

3. One solution to money problems is two people working.

c.

4. Another solution is families doing things together that don't cost money.

d.

✪✪ Complete the paragraph about financial difficulties. Use these words.

families	everything	money	managing
earning	children	share	

Money greatly influences everyone's daily lives. Many hours of each day are focused on

__earning__ money. A lack of _____ can cause anxiety and conflict for individuals
  (1)   (2)

and _____. Poverty can be especially hard on _____. They have to _____
    (3)   (4)   (5)

responsibility for the family's survival. This survival often depends on _____ a
                                           (6)

limited amount of money. Families realize that they can't have _____ they want.
                                                    (7)

They have to make hard decisions and choices.

✪✪✪ Think.

Frank has some problems that are caused by a lack of money. List some of these problems. Have you seen people like Frank in the street? What would you do if you were in that situation?

_____

_____

Check Your English

⭐ Write the correct word under each picture.

flashlight
typewriter
crib
pockets
baby
bench

1.

_____

2.

_____

3.

_____

4.

_____flashlight_____

5.

_____

6.

_____

⭐⭐ Make a question from each group of words.

1. the   picture   may   newspaper   your   take   I   for

    _May I take your picture for the newspaper?_____

2. luggage   my   borrow   trip   I   for   can   your

    _____

3. noon   if   eat   my   mind   at   do   lunch   you   I

    _____

4. kids   mind   I   mall   you   take   the   if   the   do   to

    _____

⭐⭐⭐ Finish the story. Use the words in the box. Write one word in each blank.

One day a man named Frank comes into the café. Frank is _unemployed_ and
                                                                      (1)
does not have much _____. He is very _____ and asks Katherine for
                        (2)   (3)
something to eat. Frank looks as if he has a _____ in his coat _____.
                                                  (4)   (5)
At first, everyone thinks Frank is trying to _____ the café, so they put their
                                                  (6)
hands up. After a while everyone realizes that Frank is not a _____, but
                                                                    (7)
only a man who is going through a hard time. Mr. Brashov hires Frank as the
café _____ while Jamal is on _____. Frank does very good work, so
        (8)   (9)
everyone tries to help him get a new _____. Because Frank is _____
                                          (10)   (11)
during his first job interview, he doesn't do well. He does better during his
second _____ and is offered a job as a _____. He is thankful to
            (12)   (13)
everyone and looks forward to his new job at the post office garage.

criminal
gun
handyman
hungry
interview
job
lights
lock
mechanic
money
nervous
pocket
rob
unemployed
vacation

23 The Gift

In this unit you will:

- make invitations
- read a travel brochure
- write greetings for a birthday card
- identify types of taxes

Ways to Learn

Mr. Brashov celebrates his birthday in his own *style*. In learning English, it is helpful to *know your learning style*. To *know your learning style* means to *know how you remember best*.

Know Your Learning Style

How do you learn best? Circle a, b, or c.
1. When I want to remember a new word, I . . .
    a. read it
    b. say it
    c. trace it with my finger
2. When I want to remember a person's name, I . . .
    a. see it
    b. repeat it
    c. write it many times
3. I like books with . . .
    a. pictures and words
    b. audiotapes
    c. writing exercises
4. I like to . . .
    a. read
    b. have conversations
    c. work with my hands

5. I like to learn new things by . . .
    a. watching someone else
    b. listening to someone explain
    c. doing it myself

a = seeing (with your eyes), b = listening and speaking (with your ears and voice), c = touching (with your hands)

On Your Own

Count your **a** answers. _____

Count your **b** answers. _____

Count your **c** answers. _____

How do you think you learn best? What's your learning style? _____

_____

Before You Watch

Look at the pictures. What do you see?

1.

2.

3.

4.

5.

6.

⭐ What do you see in each picture? Write the number of the picture next to the word.

___4___ bills   _____ mail

_____ balloons   _____ note

_____ keys   _____ birthday party

⭐⭐ What is happening? Write the number of the picture next to the sentence.

_____ Jess is reading a note.

_____ A man is giving Mr. Brashov a set of keys.

_____ Mr. Brashov and a man are going through the bills.

_____ Crossroads Café employees and friends are having a birthday party.

___1___ Henry is holding birthday balloons.

_____ Mr. Brashov is looking at the mail.

⭐⭐⭐ Write one question you have about each picture. Then read your questions to someone.

1. _Whose birthday is it?_ _____

2. _____

3. _____

4. _____

5. _____

6. _____

Focus For Watching   Read the questions. Then watch.

⭐ 1. Who has a birthday?
2. Who plans a surprise party?

⭐⭐ 1. Who invites Mr. Brashov to his mountain cabin?
2. Who brings a special present?

⭐⭐⭐ 1. Who writes the letter from the IRS?
2. Who do you think is the mysterious caller?

After You Watch

What do you remember? Match each question with the correct picture. You can use a picture more than once.

⭐ 1. Who has a birthday?

2. Who plans a surprise party?

✪✪ 1. Who invites Mr. Brashov to his mountain cabin?

2. Who brings a special present?

✪✪✪ 1. Who writes the letter from the IRS?

2. Who do you think is the mysterious caller?

a. Emery

b. Anna

c. Mr. Brashov

d. Jess

e. Henry, Katherine, Rosa, and Jamal

f. Joe

✪ Read the sentences. Circle Yes or No.

1. Mr. Brashov's party is a surprise.   (YES)   NO
2. Nicolae calls to say "Happy Birthday."   YES   NO
3. Mr. Brashov goes to the airport to take a vacation.   YES   NO
4. Mr. Brashov has a granddaughter.   YES   NO

✪✪ Put the sentences in order. Number 1 to 4.

_____ Joe gives Mr. Brashov the keys to his mountain cabin.

_1_ Crossroads Café employees plan a surprise birthday party.

_____ Emery helps Mr. Brashov with his bills.

_____ Mr. Brashov goes to the airport to see his daughter.

✪✪✪ Write the story. Use the four sentences above. Add these four sentences.
Then close the book and tell the story to someone.
- Mr. Brashov invites everyone to dinner as his guests.
- Mr. Brashov writes Emery a note and leaves the café.
- The cabin is open this weekend.
- The surprise party is for Mr. Brashov.

Crossroads Café employees are planning a surprise birthday party.

_____

_____

_____

_____

_____

_____

_____

_____

_____

_____

_____

_____

_____

Your New Language: Making Invitations

To invite someone you can say:
- **I'd like to invite** you **to come** to dinner.
- **Would you like to come** to dinner?
- **How about coming** to dinner with me?

To answer yes, you can say:
- **Thank you, I'd like to.**
- **Thanks, that sounds great!**

To answer no, you can say:
- **Thank you, but** I have a date.
- **I'm sorry, but** I have a date.
- **I'm afraid I can't.** I have a date.

⭐ Complete the conversations. Use these words or phrases.

wonderful   have a date   I have to   too much work

1.

I'd like to invite you to come as my guest for dinner.

I'm sorry, but I _have a date_.

2.

How about going to the lake with me on Saturday?

That sounds _____, Papa.

3.

Would you like to come with me to the cabin this weekend?

I'm afraid I can't. I have _____.

4.

How about coming to the party?

Thank you, but _____ get back to work.

 Match.

1. I'd like to invite you to have dinner with me tonight.

2. How about taking a couple of days off and coming to the mountains some time?

3. I have nothing to do this weekend.

4. When are you going to the mountains?

a. How about coming to the mountains with me?

b. Next weekend. Would you like to come along?

c. Thank you. I'd like to. What time?

d. I'm afraid I can't. I'm so busy with work, I can't get away.

Complete the conversation. Use these phrases. Write one in each blank.

I'm afraid   Thanks. I'd like to.
Would you like   How about

JESS: We're having a surprise party for Victor. __Would you like__ to come?
                                                        (1)

EMERY: _____. What time?
                (2)

JESS: You have to be here by 6:30. Victor is coming at 7:00. Joe, what are

        you doing tonight? _____ coming to the party? We've got lots
                                    (3)

        of cake.

JOE: Thanks, Jess. _____ I can't. I've got lots of work to finish tonight.
                            (4)

✪ Put the conversation in order. Number 1 to 3.

____	MR. BRASHOV:	Around 7:00 P.M.
____	JOE:	Thanks. That sounds great. What time?
1	MR. BRASHOV:	Would you like to come to my birthday party on Saturday?

✪✪ Put the conversation in order. Number 1 to 4.

____	KATHERINE:	I'm sorry. I can't. We're planning to go to the mountains that weekend.
____	ROSA:	How about coming over for dinner Friday night?
____	ROSA:	Well, how about next weekend?
____	KATHERINE:	I'm afraid I can't. I'm going to a concert that night.

✪✪✪ Put the conversation in order. Number 1 to 6.

____	JESS:	Anna, that's an excuse. Please come.
____	JESS:	Why not? Your dad would be happy to see you.
____	ANNA:	O.K. Jess. I'd really like to. It sounds great!
____	JESS:	We're having a surprise party for your dad. How about coming?
____	ANNA:	Sorry, I'd like to come, but I can't. I don't have a babysitter for Elizabeth.
____	ANNA:	Thanks, Jess. But I'm afraid I can't.

In Your Community: Travel Brochure

This is the brochure Joe showed Mr. Brashov. Answer the questions about the information on the brochure. Then tell your answers to someone.

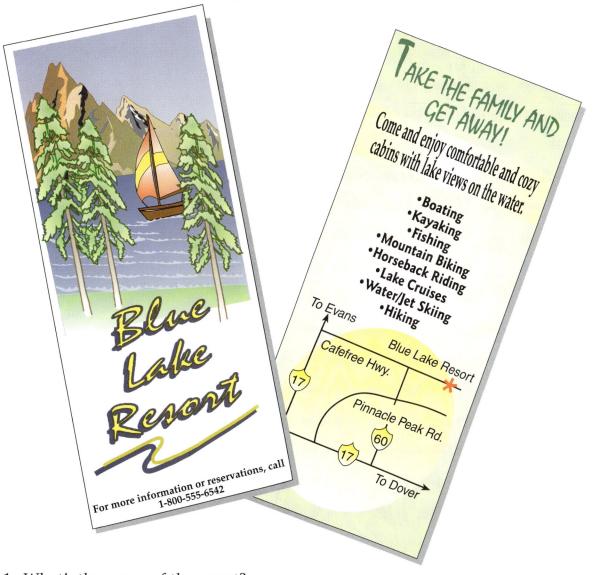

⭐ 1. What's the name of the resort? _____

2. What are three things you can do there? _____

⭐⭐ 1. If you want to stay at the resort, what should you do? _____

2. Can children go to this resort? _____ How do you know? _____

_____

⭐⭐⭐ 1. What kind of accommodations are there? _____

2. What routes can you take to get to the resort? _____

Find a travel brochure. How is it the same as or different from this travel brochure?

Read and Write: Spotlight on Mr. Brashov

Read the questions. Read the card very quickly
to find the answers. Circle the correct answers.

⭐ What kind of card is this?
   a. birthday card for a relative
   b. funny birthday card
   c. birthday card for a coworker

⭐⭐ How do the people who signed the card feel about
   Mr. Brashov's birthday?
   a. They don't care about his birthday.
   b. They are happy about his birthday.
   c. They think his birthday is funny.

⭐⭐⭐ What is the tone or feeling of this card?
   a. sympathetic   b. humorous   c. joyous

Read the card again carefully.

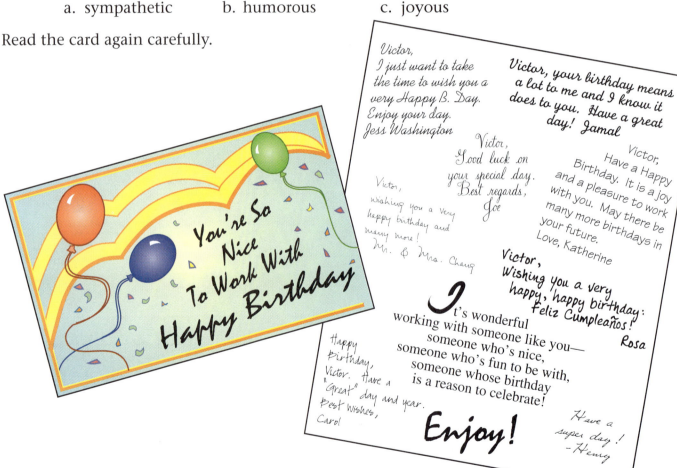

Find the word in the typed message on the card that means the same
as the word or phrase below. Write the word.

⭐ great _____

⭐⭐ to have a party _____

⭐⭐⭐ cause _____

Now you write a birthday greeting to a friend or someone you work with. Use only the words written below.

⭐ love, birthday, wonderful, happy

_____ _____! I hope
you have a _____ day.

_____,

_____
(your name)

⭐⭐ wishes, enjoy, happy, wish, special, best, birthday

I _____ you a _____
_____! _____ this
very _____ day.

_____ _____,

_____
(your name)

⭐⭐⭐ wishing, best, you, happy, very, a, day, birthday, special, regards, on, this

_____
(your name)

Read your greetings to someone. Then ask: Did you understand?
Do you have questions?

What Do You Think?

⭐ Why do you think Mr. Brashov works so many hours? Check (✓) the reasons.

☐ He doesn't speak to his daughter.

☐ Crossroads Café is very important to him.

☐ He needs the money.

☐ He likes his job.

☐ other: _____

⭐⭐ Look at the sentences below. Check (✓) I agree, I disagree, or I don't know.

	I agree.	I disagree.	I don't know.
1. Never leave till Monday what you can do on Friday.	☐	☐	☐
2. You work hard, Victor. What's wrong with giving yourself a vacation once in a while?	☐	☐	☐

⭐⭐⭐ Answer the questions. Then read your answers to someone.

1. Do you think you should never leave until tomorrow what you can do today?

_____

_____

2. What do you think is the right balance between work and relaxation in a person's life?

_____

_____

Culture Clip: Taxes

✪ Match

1. Taxes are not new.

         a.

2 We tax many things.

         b.

3. Taxes pay for services.

         c.

✪✪ Complete the sentences. Write one word in each blank. Use these words.

quality   taxes   property   benefit
earns   sales   income

Collecting taxes is not a modern idea. In ancient times taxes were collected from

conquered nations. Three types of ___taxes___ in the United States are income, property,
                                   (1)

and sales taxes. _____ taxes are paid when an individual or business _____
                (2)   (3)

money. _____ taxes provide money for cities, schools and public services.
           (4)

_____ taxes are collected when products are sold. Taxes _____ the community
    (5)   (6)

and the individual. They help maintain the _____ of life in this country.
                                          (7)

✪✪✪ Mr. Brashov asked for Emery's help because the Internal Revenue Service is
going to audit his taxes. Mr. Brashov owns a business and must pay taxes to the
government. Do you think income, property and sales taxes are all necessary taxes?
Why or why not? Write your ideas. Then tell your ideas to someone.

_____

_____

_____

_____

Check Your English

⭐ Write the correct word under each picture.

balloons
note
mail
birthday party
keys
bills

1.
_____

2.
balloons

3.
_____

4.
_____

5.
_____

6.
_____

⭐⭐ Make a sentence or question from each group of words.

1. afraid   can't   I   I'm

    _I'm afraid I can't._____

2. the   you   lake   this   like   to   to   with   go   me   would   weekend

    _____

3. dinner   guest   I'd   to   you   to   like   invite   be   my

    _____

4. movies   about   how   to   the   with   me   going   tonight

    _____

⭐⭐⭐ Finish the story. Use the words in the box. Write one word in each blank.

The employees at Crossroads Café plan a ___surprise___ birthday party for
                                        (1)

Mr. Brashov. When Mr. Brashov arrives in the morning, no one _____
                                                              (2)

him a Happy Birthday. Mr. Brashov is sad because he thinks everyone has

forgotten his _____. He _____ his employees to dinner, but no one
          (3)   (4)

can come. Joe offers Mr. Brashov _____ to his _____ for the
                           (5)   (6)

weekend. Mr. Brashov decides to go. If Mr. Brashov goes to the _____,
                                            (7)

there will be no surprise party. Jess writes a _____ from the IRS. Mr.
                                     (8)

Brashov thinks he has problems with his taxes. He must stay at Crossroads

Café and organize his _____. The Crossroads Café employees decorate
                (9)

the café with _____. What a surprise this will be for Mr. Brashov!
        (10)

balloons
bills
birthday
cabin
card
invites
keys
letter
mountains
party
surprise
wishes

24 All's Well That Ends Well

In this unit you will:

- talk about the future
- read an invitation
- write a thank you note
- describe wedding customs

Ways to Learn

Katherine has many problems the day before her wedding. The problems seem *funny* to everyone except Katherine. Mr. Brashov says, "May you always *keep your sense of humor.*" Looking for humor, or funny things, makes learning easier and more fun.

Look for Humor

Check (✓) ways you *look for humor* in learning English.

☐ I don't worry when I forget a word or phrase.
☐ I smile when someone doesn't understand me, then repeat.
☐ I listen for humor in conversations.
☐ I ask friends for help and laugh with them about mistakes.
☐ other: _____

On Your Own

The *funniest* thing about learning English is _____
_____
_____

This week, I *looked for humor* by _____
_____
_____

Before You Watch

Look at the pictures. What do you see?

1.

2.

3.

4.

5.

6.

⭐ What do you see in each picture? Write the number of the picture next to the word.

_2_ person knocking   ____ clipboard

____ wedding dress   ____ people dancing

____ taxicab   ____ tire

⭐⭐ What is happening? Write the number of the picture next to the sentence.

_5_ Henry rides in a taxicab.

____ The taxicab has a flat tire.

____ Katherine is very upset.

____ Rosa gives everyone something to do.

____ Bill knocks on the bathroom door.

____ Everyone has a good time at the party.

⭐⭐⭐ Write one question you have about each picture. Then read your questions to someone.

1. What is Rosa doing? _____

2. _____

3. _____

4. _____

5. _____

6. _____

Focus For Watching   Read the questions. Then watch.

⭐ 1. Who locks herself in the bathroom?
2. Who has a big family?
3. Who helps Katherine with her dress?

⭐⭐ 1. Who is picking up Katherine's grandfather?
2. Who loses the wedding ring?
3. Who meets his family at the café?

⭐⭐⭐ 1. Who drives the taxi?
2. Who fixes the tire?
3. Who finds the wedding ring?

After You Watch

What do you remember? Match each question with the correct picture. You can use a picture more than once.

★ 1. Who locks herself in the bathroom?

2. Who has a big family?

3. Who helps Katherine with her dress?

★★ 1. Who is picking up Katherine's grandfather?

2. Who loses the wedding ring?

3. Who meets his family at the café?

★★★ 1. Who drives the taxi?

2. Who fixes the tire?

3. Who finds the wedding ring?

a. Lars

b. Suzanne

c. Bill

d. Calli

e. Henry

f. Katherine

g. Rosa

h. Aunt Sophia

★ Read the sentences. Circle Yes or No.
1. Katherine is happy with her dress.   YES   (NO)
2. Bill's family comes to the café.   YES   NO
3. Henry rides his bike to the airport.   YES   NO
4. Lars is Bill's grandfather.   YES   NO

★★ Put the sentences in order. Number 1 to 4.

_____   However, there are many problems.

_____   Katherine gets upset about all the problems and locks herself in the bathroom.

__1__   The workers are very busy getting the café ready for a party.

_____   After a while, Katherine comes out of the bathroom and everyone has a good time at the party.

★★★ Write the story. Use the four sentences above. Add these four sentences. Then close the book and tell the story to someone.
• Also, the photographer is sick and cannot take the wedding pictures.
• While she is in the bathroom, many people come to the café for the party.
• The party is for Bill and Katherine, who are getting married.
• The airport may close because of a snowstorm.

The workers are very busy getting the café ready for a party.

_____

_____

_____

_____

_____

_____

_____

_____

_____

_____

_____

_____

_____

Your New Language: Talking about the Future

What are you going to do?

I am going to put up the decorations.

To talk about things that happen in the future, you can say:

- We are **going to make** some soup tomorrow.
- Katherine is **going to take** her kids to the movies on Saturday.

You can also say:

- I **will make** some soup tomorrow.
- Katherine **will take** her kids to the movies on Saturday.

⭐ Complete the conversations. Use these words.

be late   be   pick up   take

1.

When is the photographer going to be here?

The photographer is not going to _____be_____ here. He is sick.

2.

Where am I going?

You are going to _____ Katherine's grandfather at the airport.

3.

How are we going to get to the airport?

We are going to _____ another road.

4.

Where is my father?

Your father is going to _____ because of the snow.

✪✪ Match.

1. When is Jess going to pick up the flowers?
2. Will Lars be at the wedding?
3. When will we get to the airport?
4. Is Katherine here yet?

a. With all this snow, I don't know when. But don't worry, we'll get there.
b. He's going to pick them up at two o'clock.
c. We don't know. We don't know if his plane will get here on time.
d. No, but she will be here soon.

✪✪✪ Complete the conversation. Use these words or phrases. Write one in each blank. You may use a word or phrase more than once.

| will | are going | am going | is going |
| going to | going | | |

HENRY: Can you take me to the airport? I am ____going____ to meet someone.
                                              (1)

CALLI: Sure. I _____ to have to drive very slowly. The weather is terrible,
                   (2)
       but we _____ get there.
                 (3)

HENRY: Good. How long do you think it is _____ take?
                                              (4)

CALLI: I _____ to use different roads because of all the snow, so I don't know
           (5)
       when we _____ to get there.
                  (6)

HENRY: That's O.K. Do you know if they _____ to close the airport?
                                            (7)

CALLI: If it keeps snowing this hard, they _____ definitely close it.
                                              (8)

HENRY: I hope not. My friend is _____ get married tomorrow. If they close
                                    (9)
       the airport, her grandfather _____ miss the wedding.
                                        (10)

CALLI: Don't worry. I _____ get you there safely and you _____
                          (11)   (12)
       meet her grandfather. Everything _____ to be just fine for the
                                            (13)
       wedding.

⭐ Put the conversation in order. Number 1 to 4.

____ ROSA:	Sure, I'll help you.

_1_ ROSA:	We have a lot to do to get ready for this dinner. So what are we going to do first?

____ JAMAL:	We'll need to clean off all the tables. Then we'll have to move them around. Will you help me?

____ JAMAL:	After we finish with the tables, I am going to set up all the chairs.

⭐⭐ Put the conversation in order. Number 1 to 5.

____ CALLI:	Don't worry. You'll be safe with me. I take care of all my passengers.

____ HENRY:	That's good news. Now I'll be able to relax a little and enjoy the trip.

____ CALLI:	No problem. But there's a lot of snow out there. It's going to take a long time to get there.

____ HENRY:	I'm going to meet someone at the airport. Will you be able to get there O.K.?

____ HENRY:	That's O.K. I don't care how long it takes. I just hope we'll get there safely.

⭐⭐⭐ Put the conversation in order. Number 1 to 6.

____ KATHERINE:	I don't care. I'll come out when I feel better. But right now, I am going to stay right here.

____ BILL:	You have to. Darling, everybody is going to be here soon and they will want to meet you.

____ KATHERINE:	No, it isn't. My dress is going to look terrible. We won't have any wedding pictures because the photographer won't be here. All the snow . . . why should I come out?

____ KATHERINE:	Then they will have to use the bathroom next door!

____ BILL:	But you can't stay in there all night. You are going to have to come out sometime. When everybody gets here, someone will need to use the bathroom.

____ BILL:	Honey, will you please come out of the bathroom? Everything is going to be all right.

In Your Community: Invitations

Rosa and Mr. Brashov send invitations to the friends and family of Katherine and Bill. Answer the questions about the invitation. Then tell your answers to someone.

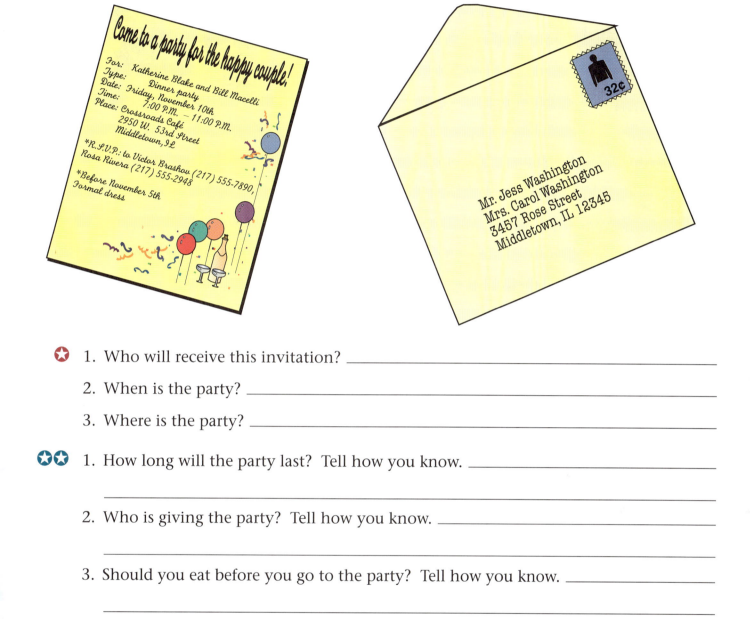

⭐ 1. Who will receive this invitation? _____

2. When is the party? _____

3. Where is the party? _____

⭐⭐ 1. How long will the party last? Tell how you know. _____

_____

2. Who is giving the party? Tell how you know. _____

_____

3. Should you eat before you go to the party? Tell how you know. _____

_____

⭐⭐⭐ 1. If you receive an invitation to this party, what should you do? _____

_____

2. Katherine's son wants to wear a T-shirt and jeans to this party. Is this appropriate?

Why or why not? _____

_____

Look in a card shop for different invitations. How are they the same as or different from this invitation?

Read and Write: Spotlight on Katherine and Bill

Bill and Katherine send thank-you notes. Read their note very quickly to find the answers. Circle the answers.

⭐ What do Bill and Katherine write about?
   a. their wedding   b. a party   c. a gift

⭐⭐ How do Katherine and Bill feel about the gift?
   a. sad   b. worried   c. happy

⭐⭐⭐ What is the tone or feeling of this letter?
   a. disappointed   b. satisfied   c. afraid

Read the note again carefully.

Dear Uncle Antonio and Aunt Sophia:
We would like to thank you both for coming to the dinner and the wedding last month. We appreciate your being there to share our special time. We would also like to thank you for the wedding card and your very generous gift. We plan to use the money you gave us to buy a television set for our new apartment.
We hope you can visit soon to eat dinner and to look at our wedding pictures. At that time you can decide which pictures you would like for your family photo album! Aunt Sophia, Katherine wants you to know that every time she looks at her wedding ring, she thinks of you. If you

didn't like pastry, she wouldn't have her ring today. Thanks again for everything. Say hello to the rest of the family for us. Stay well and we'll talk to you soon.

Love,
Bill and Katherine

Find the words in the reading. What do they mean? Circle the answer.

⭐ A **photo album** is a book for keeping:
   a. cards   b. pictures   c. records

⭐⭐ A **generous** person:
   a. likes to receive gifts   b. likes to share with others   c. spends a lot of money

⭐⭐⭐ When you **appreciate** something you:
   a. are thankful for it   b. need it   c. ask someone for it

Now you write a thank-you note to someone. In your note, include the following information.

⭐ 1. the name of the person you are writing to
   2. what the gift is
   3. what you like about the gift

⭐⭐ 1. why the person gave you the gift (birthday, wedding, baby, etc.)
    2. how you feel about the gift

⭐⭐⭐ 1. how you will use the gift
     2. news about yourself, your family, or your friends

Read your thank-you note to someone. Then ask: Did you understand?
Do you have questions?

What Do You Think?

⭐ Why do you think Katherine is upset? Check (✓) the reasons.

☐ She is afraid to meet Bill's family.

☐ Her wedding dress is too big.

☐ She doesn't want to talk to Bill.

☐ The photographer can't come to the wedding.

☐ Her wedding ring is lost.

☐ She doesn't want to see her grandfather.

⭐⭐ Look at the sentences below. Check (✓) I agree, I disagree, or I don't know.

	I agree.	I disagree.	I don't know.
1. It's not my fault I lost the ring!	☐	☐	☐
2. Calli, maybe you should drive slower in all this snow.	☐	☐	☐
3. Should we tell Antonio that he is dancing with Rosa, not Katherine?	☐	☐	☐

⭐⭐⭐ Answer the questions. Then read your answers to someone.

1. Do you think it's Suzanne's fault that she lost the ring? Tell why or why not.

_____

2. Do you think that Calli should drive slower in the snow? Tell why or why not.

_____

3. Do you think Mr. Brashov should tell Antonio that he is dancing with Rosa, not Katherine? Tell why or why not.

_____

Culture Clip: Wedding Customs

⭐ Match.

1. Cultures have special ways of celebrating special occasions like weddings.

a.

2. There are customs about the bride's clothes.

b.

3. There are also different customs for wedding gifts.

c.

⭐⭐ Complete the paragraph about wedding customs. Use these words.

groom	gifts	marriage	ceremony
family	wedding	customs	clothes
toasts			

Almost all cultures have special ways of celebrating important life events.

Traditions related to __marriage__ appear to be different in every culture. Certain
              (1)

marriage _____ are common across cultures. Many hours are spent preparing for
        (2)

a _____ and the special _____ the bride will wear. Friends and _____
  (3)   (4)   (5)

from near and far join the festivities. They bring _____ to celebrate the new
                (6)

union of the bride and _____. The festivities include special food, music, and
           (7)

dancing and _____ to the bride and groom. The wedding _____ is a joyful
      (8)   (9)

occasion. It marks the beginning of a new family and hope for the future.

⭐⭐⭐ Think.

Katherine and Bill have special ways of celebrating their wedding. How are weddings celebrated in your culture? Write your ideas. Then tell your ideas to someone.

_____

_____

Check Your English

⭐ Write the correct word under each picture.

wedding dress

tire

taxicab

person
   knocking

people
   dancing

clipboard

1.

_____

2.

_____

3.

_____

4.

_____

5.

_____

6.

wedding dress

⭐⭐ Make a sentence or question from each group of words.

1. snow   to   a   lot   we   are   have   going   of

   We are going to have a lot of snow. OR _Are we going to have a lot of snow?_

2. party   arrive   at   Lars   the   will   late

   _____

3. are   married   tomorrow   to   Bill   going   Katherine   and   get

   _____

4. Katherine   toast   Mr. Brashov   a   make   and   will   Bill   to

   _____

⭐⭐⭐ Finish the story. Use the words in the box. Write one word in each blank.

The workers are getting ready for a party. The party is for Bill and Katherine,
who are going to get ___married___. But there are many _____. There is a
                              (1)   (2)
bad _____ and the _____ may close. Katherine gets upset because
     (3)   (4)
her _____ is coming by airplane. She is also _____ because the
    (5)   (6)
_____ is sick and will not be able to take the pictures at the _____.
 (7)   (8)
Another problem is that her _____ is too big. Because she gets upset
                                    (9)
about all these problems, she locks herself in the _____. While she is in
                                                     (10)
the bathroom, many people _____ at the party. After a while, Katherine
                                   (11)
comes out of the bathroom and is _____ to meet Bill's _____. For
                                    (12)   (13)
the rest of the evening, everyone has a good time.

airport
arrive
bathroom
decorations
family
grandfather
happy
married
photographer
problems
sad
snowstorm
taxicab
wedding
wedding dress

25 Comings and Goings

In this unit you will:

- talk about future plans and possibilities
- read a school application
- write a thank-you note
- describe reasons for staying in the United States

Ways to Learn

Katherine and Henry are getting ready to make changes. They need *encouragement* and *compliments*. In language learning, it is important to *tell yourself you are doing well*.

Compliment Yourself

I *compliment* or *encourage* myself by . . .

☐ making positive statements to myself (*good job! nice work!* . . .)

☐ writing notes to myself, posting the notes on mirrors (*good work this week! you did it!* . . .)

☐ writing successes in a small notebook (*On 2/3/97, I called my son's teacher.*)

☐ rewarding myself (*a snack, a study break, a new book* . . .)

☐ telling others about my successes (*a teacher, a friend, a coworker, family* . . .)

☐ marking lessons well done in the textbook (*with a star ★ or a check mark ✓*)

☐ other: _____

On Your Own

Last week, I *complimented* myself by _____

_____

I need to *encourage* myself more often.	YES	NO
It's easier to *compliment* others.	YES	NO

Before You Watch

Look at the pictures. What do you see?

1.

2.

3.

4.

5.

6.

⭐ What do you see in each picture? Write the number of the picture next to the word.

<u> 2 </u> dinner guest   ____ cash register

____ gift   ____ CD (compact disc)

____ singer   ____ sad people

⭐⭐ What is happening? Write the number of the picture next to the sentence.

<u> 4 </u> Katherine teaches a woman to use the cash register.

____ Katherine and Suzanne open a gift.

____ The man listens to a lot of CDs in his office.

____ The guests at the party become sad.

____ Henry's band plays at Crossroads Café.

____ Jamal and Jihan have dinner with a friend.

⭐⭐⭐ Write one question you have about each picture. Then read your questions to someone.

1. <u>Who is the man at the desk?</u> _____

2. _____

3. _____

4. _____

5. _____

6. _____

Focus For Watching   Read the questions. Then watch.

⭐ 1. Who leaves a job at the café?
  2. Who wants a record contract?
  3. Who is the new worker at the café?

⭐⭐ 1. Who listens to a tape of the band?
  2. Who interviews people for a job?
  3. Who offers Jamal a job?

⭐⭐⭐ 1. Who wants to return home?
  2. Who tells everyone at the café the bad news?
  3. Who is the bad news about?

After You Watch

What do you remember? Match each question with the correct picture. You can use a picture more than once.

★ 1. Who leaves a job at the café?

2. Who wants a record contract?

3. Who is the new worker at the café?

★★ 1. Who listens to a tape of the band?

2. Who interviews people for a job?

3. Who offers Jamal a job?

★★★ 1. Who wants to return home?

2. Who tells everyone at the café the bad news?

3. Who is the bad news about?

a. Abdullah

b. Mr. Brashov

c. Henry

d. Danny

e. Jess

f. Katherine

g. Jamal

h. Marie

⭐ Read the sentences. Circle Yes or No.

1. Katherine is happy about Marie's work.   (YES)   NO
2. Jess and Carol come to Katherine's party.   YES   NO
3. Abdullah is coming to work in the United States. YES   NO
4. Henry gets a music contract from Mr. Finkelman.   YES   NO

✪✪ Put the sentences in order. Number 1 to 4.

_____ Katherine quits her job and helps find a new waitress.

_____ Everyone at the party becomes sad when Mr. Brashov gets
a phone call from Carol Washington.

_____ The café workers have a going-away party for Katherine.

__1__ The workers at Crossroads Café make changes in their lives.

✪✪✪ Write the story. Use the four sentences above. Add these four sentences.
Then close the book and tell the story to someone.

• Jamal is offered an engineering job.
• Carol tells Mr. Brashov that Jess was in a car accident and he died.
• Henry and his band play their music for a record producer.
• Besides Katherine, Henry and Jamal also are given chances to make
changes in their jobs.

The workers at Crossroads Café make changes in their lives. Katherine quits her job and

helps find a new waitress.

_____

_____

_____

_____

_____

_____

_____

_____

_____

_____

Your New Language: Talking about Future Plans and Possibilities

Mr. Brashov, why are you so happy?

I'm going to take a little vacation next month.

When you are sure something is going to happen, you can say:

- I **am going to** study music at school.
- Mr. Brashov **is going to** take a little vacation.
- They **aren't going to** see a movie tonight.

When you are not sure if something is going to happen you can say:

- I **might** study music at school.
- Mr. Brashov **might** visit his daughter.
- They **might** not see a movie tonight.

⭐ Complete the conversations. Use these words.

| ask | win | play | arrive |

1.

When is the band going to play?

We are going to ___play___ at nine o'clock.

2.

What are you going to do about the job?

I am going to _____ Abdullah for more information.

3.

What time is Katherine's party?

Everyone is going to _____ at eight o'clock.

4.

Why does Jess look so happy?

He is going to _____ this chess game.

✪✪ Match.

1. What are you going to do tomorrow?
2. When is Henry's concert?
3. Can you go to the movies tonight?
4. What is Jamal going to do?

a. He might accept a job in Egypt.
b. I'm going to go shopping.
c. I don't know. I have a math test tomorrow. I might have to study.
d. The band will play at nine o'clock.

✪✪✪ Complete the conversation. Use these words or phrases. Write one in each blank. You may use a word or phrase more than once.

going to go   am going to   are going to   might

KATHERINE: I am ___going to go___ home in a few minutes. May I talk to you for
                                    (1)
               a moment, please?

MR. BRASHOV: Sure. Let's sit down at the table here.

KATHERINE: I need to tell you something. I _____ leave Crossroads Café
                                                         (2)
               in a couple of weeks.

MR. BRASHOV: Why? Is there a problem?

KATHERINE: Oh, no. Everything is fine. I've decided that I _____ go back
                                                                    (3)
               to school.

MR. BRASHOV: Oh, that's wonderful news. Do you know what you _____
                                                                         (4)
               study?

KATHERINE: I'm not sure, but I _____ study law. I have always wanted
                                          (5)
               to be a lawyer.

MR. BRASHOV: I am glad about your decision to go back to school. But I _____
                                                                              (6)
               miss you. And I think Rosa _____ miss you, too.
                                                 (7)

⭐ Put the conversation in order. Number 1 to 4.

_____ JAMAL: What else do you think you might do?

_____ KATHERINE: First of all, I will spend more time with my kids.

__1__ JAMAL: What are you going to do?

_____ KATHERINE: I might go to school.

⭐⭐ Put the conversation in order. Number 1 to 6.

_____ HENRY: Yes, but you will really like our music.

_____ DANNY: Yes. Give me a call tomorrow. I am going to be out of the office in the morning, but I should be back around two o'clock.

_____ DANNY: I might. You know I listen to a lot of bands just like you.

_____ DANNY: Maybe that's true, but I have a business meeting in about fifteen minutes. I might have some time later this afternoon to listen to it.

_____ HENRY: Are you going to listen to our tape?

_____ HENRY: Oh. So, should we call you?

⭐⭐⭐ Put the conversation in order. Number 1 to 7.

_____ MR. BRASHOV: I don't know, but I am going to miss her. We're all a big family here.

_____ JESS: What's the matter, Victor? You look worried.

_____ MR. BRASHOV: Well, for one thing, Katherine is leaving us. She says she's going to spend more time with her kids, and she thinks she might go to law school.

_____ JESS: That's wonderful. But what are you going to do without Katherine?

_____ MR. BRASHOV: I hope you are going to keep coming in even after Katherine leaves. I might get bored if I don't get the chance to beat you in chess.

_____ JESS: That's the truth. That's why I enjoy coming here so much.

_____ JESS: Don't worry, my friend. I'll be drinking coffee here for a long, long time.

In Your Community: School Applications

Katherine fills out an application for school. Answer the questions about the application. Then tell your answers to someone.

To the applicant: Please answer the questions on this application. Put a check (✓) in the boxes for your answer. A fee of $30.00 paid by check is required with each application.

Application Deadline: February 1 (Fall semester) September 15 (Spring semester)

1. Please check (✓) one: ☐ Mr. ☐ Miss ☑ Ms. ☐ Mrs.
2. <u>Blake Macelli</u> / <u>Katherine</u> / <u>S</u>
    Last name   First Name   M.I.
*3. Age <u>35</u>
4. Address <u>34 Lincoln Avenue, Apt. 108</u>   <u>Middletown, IL</u>   <u>12345</u>
                City   State   Zip Code
*5. Sex: ☐ Male ☑ Female
6. Home Telephone: (<u>2 1 7</u>) <u>5 5 5</u> - <u>4 2 0 6</u>
                   area code
7. Are you a U.S. citizen? ☑ Yes ☐ No
8. Are you an Illinois resident? ☑ Yes ☐ No
9. Family Income: <u>$32,500</u>
10. Number in family (including applicant): <u>4</u>
*11. Race/Ethnicity (✓ one box): ☑ White, non Hispanic ☐ Black, non Hispanic ☐ Asian/ Pacific Islander
                             ☐ Native American ☐ Hispanic/Latino ☐ Not listed above
12. Full-time or part-time study? ☑ Full-time ☐ Part-time
13. New student or transfer student? ☐ New ☑ Transfer
14. College you attended: <u>Carleton College, Minnesota</u>
15. High School—Did you: ☑ Graduate ☐ Withdraw ☐ Complete the G.E.D.

Student signature <u>*Katherine Blake Macelli*</u> Date <u>2/16</u>
* optional question

✪ 1. Does she want to go to school full-time or part-time? _____

2. Did Katherine go to college before? _____

3. What is Katherine's middle initial? _____

✪✪ 1. Which questions doesn't Katherine have to answer? _____

2. Does Katherine have a G.E.D.? Tell how you know. _____

    _____

3. Does Katherine have to send anything with her application? If so, what?

    _____

✪✪✪ 1. Will Katherine be able to start school in the fall? Tell why or why not.

    _____

2. Katherine may get financial aid from the state to help her pay for school. A family of four can get help if their income is less than $23,200 a year. Can Katherine receive any money? Tell why or why not. _____

Look at two school applications. How are they the same as or different from Katherine's application?

Read and Write: Spotlight on Katherine

Read the questions. Read Katherine's card very quickly to find the answers. Circle the answers.

⭐ What does Katherine write about?
a. her kids and her husband
b. her feelings about Mr. Brashov
c. her plans about going to school

⭐⭐ How does Katherine feel about Mr. Brashov?
a. She is glad that he won't be her boss anymore.
b. She really likes Mr. Brashov and will miss him.
c. She thinks of him as only her boss.

⭐⭐⭐ What is the tone or feeling of this letter?
a. thankful   b. hopeful   c. worried

Read the card again carefully.

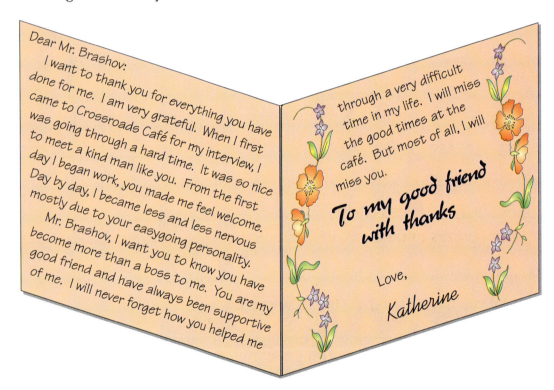

Dear Mr. Brashov:
I want to thank you for everything you have done for me. I am very grateful. When I first came to Crossroads Café for my interview, I was going through a hard time. It was so nice to meet a kind man like you. From the first day I began work, you made me feel welcome. Day by day, I became less and less nervous mostly due to your easygoing personality.
Mr. Brashov, I want you to know you have become more than a boss to me. You are my good friend and have always been supportive of me. I will never forget how you helped me

through a very difficult time in my life. I will miss the good times at the café. But most of all, I will miss you.

To my good friend with thanks

Love,

Katherine

Find the words in the reading. What do they mean? Circle the answer.

⭐ **Nervous:**
a. ready   b. worried   c. well-paid

⭐⭐ **Grateful:**
a. thankful   b. happy   c. angry

⭐⭐⭐ **Supportive:**
a. hard working   b. intelligent   c. helpful

Now you write a friendly note to thank someone who is special to you. In your note, include the following information.

⭐ 1. the name of the person you are writing to
2. why you are writing to the person
3. your signature

✪✪ 1. how you feel about the person
2. what you like about this person
3. what the person has done for you

✪✪✪ 1. why this person is so special to you
2. a closing (love, sincerely)

To my good friend with thanks

Read your friendly note to someone. Then ask: Did you understand? Do you have questions?

What Do You Think?

✪ Why do you think Jamal wants to go back to Egypt? Check (✓) the reasons.

☐ He wants to work as an engineer.

☐ He likes the weather there.

☐ He feels his life is getting better here.

☐ He can't keep working as a handyman.

☐ He doesn't feel much like a man.

☐ Egypt is his home.

✪✪ Look at the sentences below. Check (✓) I agree, I disagree, or I don't know.

	I agree.	I disagree.	I don't know.
1. *Victor, you should slow down and leave time for important things.*	☐	☐	☐
2. *Dropping out of school is something you will regret.*	☐	☐	☐
3. *A friend respects whatever work you do.*	☐	☐	☐

✪✪✪ Answer the questions. Then read your answers to someone.

1. Do you think people should slow down and leave time for important things? Tell why or why not.

_____

2. Do you think that dropping out of school is something to regret? Tell why or why not.

_____

3. Do you think you should respect whatever work your friends do? Tell why or why not.

_____

Culture Clip: Returning to Your Home Culture

⭐ Match.

1. I would have to start from ground zero.

2. I don't fit in there any more.

3. I am used to the American way of doing business.

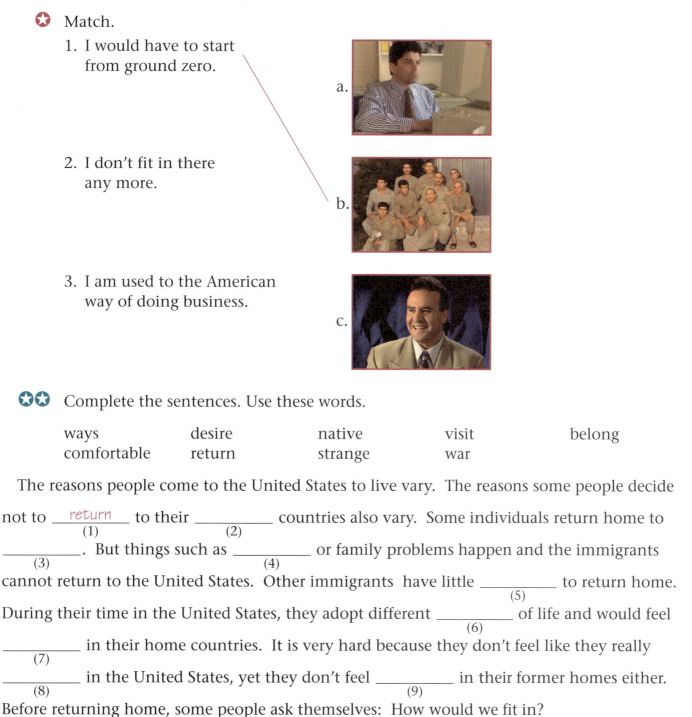

a.

b.

c.

⭐⭐ Complete the sentences. Use these words.

ways	desire	native	visit	belong
comfortable	return	strange	war	

The reasons people come to the United States to live vary. The reasons some people decide

not to ___return___ to their _____ countries also vary. Some individuals return home to
　　　(1)　　　　　　　　　(2)

_____. But things such as _____ or family problems happen and the immigrants
　(3)　　　　　　　　　　　　　　(4)

cannot return to the United States. Other immigrants have little _____ to return home.
　　　　　　　　　　　　　　　　　　　　　　　　　　　　　　　　(5)

During their time in the United States, they adopt different _____ of life and would feel
　　　　　　　　　　　　　　　　　　　　　　　　　　　　　　　(6)

_____ in their home countries. It is very hard because they don't feel like they really
　(7)

_____ in the United States, yet they don't feel _____ in their former homes either.
　(8)　　　　　　　　　　　　　　　　　　　　　(9)

Before returning home, some people ask themselves: How would we fit in?

⭐⭐⭐ Think.

Jamal and Jihan have trouble deciding whether to move back to their home country to live. What would you do if you were in their position? List some advantages and disadvantages of your decision.

_____

_____

Check Your English

⭐ Write the correct word under each picture.

dinner guest
sad people
singer
gift
cash register
CD (compact disc)

1.

_____

2.

_____

3.

dinner guest

4.

_____

5.

_____

6.

_____

⭐⭐ Make a sentence or question from each group of words.

1. going   a   contract   get   Henry   to   is   record

Henry is going to get a record contract. OR Is Henry going to get a record contract?

2. Egypt   and   back   are   Jihan   going   to   Jamal   move   to

_____

3. game   big   Jess   chess   win   the   might

_____

4. lawyer   a   become   Katherine   might

_____

⭐⭐⭐ Finish the story. Use the words in the box. Write one word in each blank.

A lot of things happen at Crossroads Café. Some of the __<u>workers</u>__ make
(1)
_____ in their jobs. Katherine quits her _____ job because she
(2)   (3)
wants to go back to _____. Henry and his _____ play their music
(4)   (5)
for a _____ producer. The producer likes the music, but does not give
(6)
them a record _____. Jamal's friend Abdullah offers Jamal an
(7)
engineering job in _____. Jamal and Jihan _____ the job, but can't
(8)   (9)
_____ what they will do. The café workers have a _____ to say
(10)   (11)
good-bye to Katherine. They are _____ until Mr. Brashov gets a phone
(12)
call from Carol Washington. Carol tells Mr. Brashov that Jess _____ in a
(13)
car accident. Everyone is sad; the café just won't be the same without Jess.

band
changes
contract
decide
died
discuss
Egypt
happy
hire
must
party
record
school
waitress
workers

26 Winds of Change

In this unit you will:

- talk about necessity
- read a schedule
- write a good-bye letter
- identify goals

Ways to Learn

Everyone at Crossroads Café is moving on. The employees are *evaluating* their learning and making changes. At the end of a course, it is important to *evaluate your learning*.

Evaluate Your Learning

What can you do in English? Fill in the blanks with **3, 2, 1,** or **NA**.

> 3 = often   2 = sometimes
> 1 = never   NA = doesn't apply

___ I have conversations.
___ I use what I learned.
___ I feel confident talking to my supervisor at work.
___ I write notes, letters, and fill out forms.
___ I understand English without translation to my language.
___ I feel comfortable at events where people speak English.
___ other: _____

On Your Own

The most valuable thing I learned from Crossroads Café was _____

_____

My favorite lesson was _____

because _____

_____

I will be able to use _____

_____

_____

_____

Before You Watch

Look at the pictures. What do you see?

1.

2.

3.

4.

5.

6.

⭐ What do you see in each picture? Write the number of the picture next to the word.

__6__ happy people   _____ envelope

_____ college catalogue   _____ chess board

_____ carton   _____ bandage

⭐⭐ What is happening? Write the number of the picture next to the sentence.

__4__ Carol gives Mr. Brashov an envelope.

_____ Jamal packs his tools in a shipping carton.

_____ Rosa and Mr. Brashov are happy.

_____ Marie puts a bandage on Henry's hand.

_____ Mr. Brashov gives the chess board to Carol.

_____ Rosa and Henry look at Katherine's college catalogue.

⭐⭐⭐ Write one question you have about each picture. Then read your questions to someone.

1. _Why is Jamal putting his tools in a carton?_ _____

2. _____

3. _____

4. _____

5. _____

6. _____

Focus For Watching   Read the questions. Then watch.

⭐ 1. Who does Mr. Brashov miss?
2. Who is angry with Henry?
3. Who gets hurt at the café?

⭐⭐ 1. Who comes to visit the café and helps out?
2. Who gives Mr. Brashov tickets for a trip?
3. Who is the new manager of the café?

⭐⭐⭐ 1. Who helps Carol?
2. Who wants to buy the café?
3. Who decides to go to the same school as Katherine?

After You Watch

What do you remember? Match each question with the correct picture. You can use a picture more than once.

⭐ 1. Who does Mr. Brashov miss?

a. Derek

2. Who is angry with Henry?

b. Henry

3. Who gets hurt at the café?

c. Carol

⭐⭐ 1. Who comes to visit the café and helps out?

d. Marie

2. Who gives Mr. Brashov tickets for a trip?

e. Jess

3. Who is the new manager of the café?

f. Mr. Clayborne

⭐⭐⭐ 1. Who helps Carol?

g. Rosa

2. Who wants to buy the café?

h. Katherine

3. Who decides to go to the same school as Katherine?

★ Read the sentences. Circle Yes or No.

1. Mr. Clayborne is the new café manager.　　YES　　(NO)
2. Henry decides to go to college.　　YES　　NO
3. Mr. Brashov sells the café.　　YES　　NO
4. Carol goes on a trip with her son.　　YES　　NO

★★ Put the sentences in order. Number 1 to 4.

_____　Mr. Brashov thinks about selling the café.

_____　In addition to Jamal, Jihan, and Mr. Brashov, Henry makes a decision that will change his life.

__1__　The Crossroads Café workers make decisions about the future.

_____　For example, Jamal and Jihan decide about Jamal's job offer in Egypt.

★★★ Write the story. Use the four sentences above. Add these four sentences. Then close the book and tell the story to someone.

- He meets with a businessman who wants to buy the café.
- He finally decides not to sell and asks Rosa to be the new manager.
- Although Henry still loves music, he decides to go to college to expand his opportunities for the future.
- They finally decide that Egypt is their home and they can have a good life there.

The Crossroads Café workers make decisions about the future. For example, Jamal and Jihan have to decide about Jamal's job offer in Egypt.

_____

_____

_____

_____

_____

_____

_____

_____

_____

_____

_____

Your New Language: Talking about Necessity

When you have an obligation, you can say:

- I **have to leave** now.
- Carol **has to do** a lot of paperwork.
- Katherine **has to take** a few more classes before she starts law school.

You can also say:

- I **must leave** now.
- Carol **must do** a lot of paperwork.
- Katherine **must take** a few more classes before she starts law school.

⭐ Complete the conversations. Use these words.

take　　　　　stay　　　　　keep　　　　　buy

1.

I'm going home now.

You can't go home. You have to ___stay___.

2.

What are you doing today?

I have to _____ our plane tickets.

3.

What's in the bag?

It's the chess set. You have to _____ it here.

4.

How many classes do you have to _____?

I'm not sure. I have to talk with someone at the college.

⭐⭐ Match.

1. Do I have to get stitches in my hand?
2. Why aren't you a nurse now?
3. I have to leave now.
4. You must take some time off from the café.

a. So do I. I'll walk out with you.
b. I don't think I can do that now. It's too busy.
c. No, but you must keep it clean.
d. I must go back to school to get a certificate for this country.

⭐⭐⭐ Complete the conversation. Use these words. Write one word in each blank. You may use a word more than once.

try   be   must   come
keep   have

MR. BRASHOV: Hi, Carol. I wanted to see how you were doing. I don't want to disturb you.

CAROL: Victor, please ___come___ in and sit for awhile. It's so good
(1)

to see you.

MR. BRASHOV: I can't stay too long. I _____ to get back to the café. I just
(2)

wanted to give you something.

CAROL: Oh, it's Jess's chess set. Oh, how he loved to play! But, Victor, you have

to_____ it. Jess would want it that way.
(3)

MR. BRASHOV: No, Carol, I can't. Jess told me that you gave him the chess set when

he retired. You _____ keep it here where it belongs.
(4)

CAROL: Did you know that Jess taught me to play chess? But I don't think I could ever play again.

MR. BRASHOV: I know what you mean, Carol. But we have to _____ to
(5)

remember all the happy times we had with Jess. He _____
(6)

continue to be a part of us even though he's gone.

CAROL: Yes, I know. I have to _____ strong. But it's just so hard to
(7)

think about Jess without feeling sad.

✪ Put the conversation in order. Number 1 to 4.

____	JIHAN:	Why? Is there a problem at the café?
____	JAMAL:	Oh, I have to work late tomorrow night.
_1_	JIHAN:	What's the matter, Jamal?
____	JAMAL:	Yes. I have to replace some parts in the heating system.

✪✪ Put the conversation in order. Number 1 to 6.

____	HENRY:	I know, but I had to do the dishes in a hurry. One of the glasses broke in the sink. I can't stop the bleeding.
____	HENRY:	Thank you. Is there anything more I have to do?
____	MARIE:	You must be more careful.
____	HENRY:	Oh great! I cut my hand!
____	MARIE:	No, not really. But you must keep it clean and dry.
____	MARIE:	You can't? Let me take a look. I don't think you will have to get stitches. I'll just put a bandage on it for now.

✪✪✪ Put the conversation in order. Number 1 to 8.

____	KATHERINE:	I have to take a math class and a writing class. I can choose the others.
____	ROSA:	Why? Can't Bill watch the kids at night?
____	KATHERINE:	Oh, it's the catalogue from City College. I have to choose some classes.
____	KATHERINE:	No, I must take classes during the day when my kids are at school.
____	ROSA:	What are you reading?
____	KATHERINE:	Sometimes Bill has to work at night. And I really can't afford a babysitter very often.
____	ROSA:	What classes are you thinking about?
____	ROSA:	Are they night classes?

In Your Community: Campus Map

Here is a map of Katherine's school. Answer the questions about the map. Then tell your answers to someone.

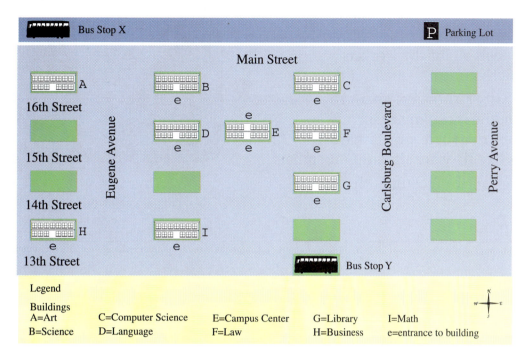

1. How many school buildings are shown on this map? _____

2. What is in building G? _____

3. If you are going to study law, in which building will you spend a lot of time?

   _____

4. What building is on the corner of Carlsburg Boulevard and Main Street? _____

1. Which bus stop is closer to the Math building? _____

2. Can you enter any building on Carlsburg Boulevard? Tell how you know.

   _____

1. How is the Campus Center different from the other buildings? _____

   _____

2. If you get off the bus at Bus Stop X, which direction do you have to walk to get to

   the library? _____

   _____

Look at a map of a school campus, shopping center, or other area. How is it the same as or different from the map of Katherine's school?

Read and Write: Spotlight on Mr. Brashov

Read the questions. Read Mr. Brashov's farewell letter very quickly to find the answers. Circle the answers.

⭐ What does Mr. Brashov write about?
   a. how he will spend his time now
   b. how he feels about the workers
   c. how much money he made at the café

⭐⭐ How does Mr. Brashov feel about the workers?
   a. He is glad he is leaving them.
   b. He wishes they had worked harder for him.
   c. He feels like they are all family members.

⭐⭐⭐ What is the tone or feeling of this letter?
   a. worried   b. scared   c. satisfied

Read the letter again carefully.

My dear friends:

Tomorrow I leave on my trip with my family. Before I go, I want to express my feelings toward all of you. I hope you enjoyed working at Crossroads Café. I certainly enjoyed being your boss. I felt we were a family here. I am going to miss that a great deal.

I decided to say good-bye to the café mainly because of Jess. He always said that I should enjoy life more. When he died, I thought about my own life. I realized that there are more important things in life than work.

To Rosa: I hope everything goes well for you at the café and at school. I know you will do a terrific job!

To Jamal: Good luck with your engineering job and your new life in Egypt. I wish you, Jihan, and Azza much health and happiness.

To Katherine: May you, Bill, and the kids be very happy. Best of luck in school. You will be a great lawyer!

To Henry: Best of luck in college. I hope you never give up your dream of being a musician. Remember that our dreams are one of the few things we can really call our own.

Thanks again for all your hard work. I will miss you all.

   Love, Victor Brashov

Find the words in the reading. What do they mean? Circle the answer.

⭐ A **dream** is something that:
   a. costs a lot of money   b. you wish or hope for   c. you read about

⭐⭐ When you **express** something, you:
   a. tell about it   b. carry it   c. use it

⭐⭐⭐ When you **realize** something, you:
   a. think about it   b. write about it   c. start to understand it

Now you write a good-bye letter. In your letter include the following information.

⭐ 1. the name of the person you are writing to
　　 2. why you are writing the letter
　　 3. your signature

⭐⭐ 1. the reason(s) you are saying good-bye
　　　2. how you feel about the person
　　　3. some experience you and the person had together

⭐⭐⭐ 1. what you will miss about the person
　　　　2. your best wishes about something in the future

Read your good-bye letter to someone. Then ask: Did you understand?
Do you have questions?

What Do You Think?

⭐ Why does Mr. Brashov leave Crossroads Café? Check (✓) the reasons.

☐ He wants to get another job.

☐ He needs to make more money.

☐ He wants to spend time with his family.

☐ He wants to start enjoying his life.

☐ He thinks about what Jess told him about taking time off.

☐ He wants to open another café.

☐ other: _____

⭐⭐ Look at the sentences below. Check (✓) I agree, I disagree, or I don't know.

	I agree.	I disagree.	I don't know.
1. Both of us should make this decision.	☐	☐	☐
2. There aren't many opportunities for a busboy with a high school education.	☐	☐	☐
3. Don't wait for the perfect time to do things in your life; it may never come.	☐	☐	☐

⭐⭐⭐ Answer the questions. Then read your answers to someone.

1. When a decision involves a couple, should they make the decision together?
Tell why or why not.

_____

2. Do you think there are many opportunities for a busboy with a high school
education? Tell why or why not.

_____

3. Do you think you should wait for the perfect time to do things in life? Tell why
or why not.

_____

Culture Clip: Achieving Goals

⭐ Match.

1. Edgar's first job, working in a restaurant, helped pay for his college education.

a.

2. After college, Edgar worked to buy things like his house.

b.

3. Now, Edgar has a job helping children.

c.

⭐⭐ Complete the paragraph about achieving goals. Use these words.

meaning	goals	student	English	radio
graduation	degrees	employee	children	

During people's lives, their goals may change. Edgar Vallarmin is an example. After his <u>graduation</u> from high school, Edgar left Colombia for the United States. When he
(1)

arrived, he enrolled in a class to learn _____. For the next few years, he was a full-
(2)

time _____ and a full-time _____. After Edgar got his _____ he began to
(3)   (4)   (5)

make a name for himself. He worked long hours, met the right people, and hosted a

_____ show. Then his _____ changed; he was successful, but could not see
(6)   (7)

real _____ in his work. So he became the director of "Big Brothers," an
(8)

organization for _____ who do not have fathers.
(9)

⭐⭐⭐ Think.

Like Edgar, workers at Crossroads Café have changed their goals. How about your goals? List your past goals and what you did to achieve them. Then list your current goals and what you are doing to achieve them. Share your lists with someone.

_____

_____

Check Your English

⭐ Write the correct word under each picture.

college
   catalogue

carton

envelope

happy people

bandage

chess board

1.
_____

2.
_____

3.
college catalogue

4.
_____

5.
_____

6.
_____

⭐⭐ Make a sentence from each group of words.

1. doctor   sick   baby   to   the   has   take   he   his   to

    He has to take his sick baby to the doctor.

2. decision   Henry   about   make   must   school   a

_____

3. has   bus   ride   every   the   brother   work   to   my   to   day

_____

4. get   hard   to   student   grades   study   a   must   good

_____

⭐⭐⭐ Finish the story. Use the words in the box. Write one word in each blank.

Everyone at Crossroads Café makes decisions about the future. Mr. Brashov

says __good-bye__ to the café. He wants to _____ more time with his family.
    (1)   (2)

He asks Rosa to be the café _____. Rosa is happy with Mr. Brashov's
                        (3)

_____ and accepts the job. Jamal _____ an engineering position
(4)   (5)

in Egypt. He and Jihan _____ that they could have a good life back home.
                 (6)

Katherine goes back to school to _____ law. Her dream is to become a
                    (7)

_____. Henry also makes a decision about his life. He decides that he
(8)

wants to go to _____. It seems that everyone at the café listened to what
          (9)

Carol Washington _____ them: "Life is too short. Don't _____ for
            (10)   (11)

the perfect _____ to do things with your life. That day may never come."
       (12)

| accepts |
| college |
| cook |
| decide |
| decision |
| dream |
| good-bye |
| lawyer |
| manager |
| repair |
| spend |
| study |
| time |
| told |
| wait |

Teacher/Tutor Appendix

If you have read the section *To the Learner* at the beginning of this book, the information in this appendix will provide a more detailed understanding of the scope and the goals of the program. The *Crossroads Café* print and video materials are closely correlated to provide everything needed for successful, non-stressful language-learning experiences, either alone or with a teacher or tutor.

The *Worktexts*

The two *Crossroads Café Worktexts* provide multi-level language activities with three levels of challenge: Beginning High, Intermediate Low, and Intermediate High as defined by the ESL Model Standards for Adult Education Programs (Sacramento: California Department of Education, 1992); or SPL 4, 5, and 6 as defined in the competency-based, Mainstream English Language Training (MELT) Resource Package (Washington, DC: Office of Refugee Resettlement, 1985). These activities are visually designated in the *Worktext* as ⭐, ⭐⭐, or ⭐⭐⭐, respectively. The 1-star exercises ask learners to communicate using words and phrases; responses are frequently based on a visual stimulus. The 2-star exercises ask learners to communicate using learned phrases and structures; responses may be based on visual stimulus or text. The 3-star exercises are designed for students who can participate in basic conversation; responses are most often based on text, not visuals. *Worktext* unit exercises develop *story comprehension, language skills,* and *higher order thinking* and they provide practice in reading, writing, and speaking. Every *Worktext* unit opens with a photo depicting the theme of the storyline, a list of learning objectives, and a learning strategy.

Crossroads Café Worktext Framework

	Exercise Section	Purpose	⭐	⭐⭐	⭐⭐⭐
Story Comprehension (Video)	*Before You Watch*	Preview story-line vocabulary and events.	Match words with video photos to highlight key plot points.	Match sentences with photos.	Write a question about each photo.
	Focus for Watching	Provide story focus.	Answer questions about elements of main plot.	Answer additional questions about main plot.	Answer additional questions focused on details of story.
	After You Watch	Check story comprehension.	Answer yes/no questions about the story plot using same content as previous two exercises.	Arrange 3–6 sentences about story in proper sequence.	Add, in the appropriate place, 3–4 new sentences providing additional detail.
Language Development	*Your New Language*	Focus on language function and grammatical structure of the "Word Play" video segment, e.g., making promises: *I promise to. . ., I promise that I will. . . .*	Copy words or phrases into sentences conveying language functions.	Match 2 parts of 2-line exchanges, e.g., question-answer, statement-response.	Complete a fill-in-the-blank dialogue with correct grammatical structures.

	Exercise Section	Purpose	★	★★	★★★
	Discourse Exercise	Enable learners to see language flow.	Sequence a dialogue of 3–4 sentences.	Sequence a dialogue of 4–6 sentences.	Sequence a dialogue of 6–8 sentences.
	In Your Community	Develop reading skills using reading materials from the community, e.g., a lease.	Answer factual questions taken directly from reading.	Answer factual questions requiring synthesis.	Answer questions requiring inference.
	Read and Write	Develop reading skills	Identify main idea.	Identify factual details.	Identify tone or feeling.
		Determine meaning from context.	Identify words/ phrases with same meaning.	Identify words/ phrases that are clues to meaning.	Infer word meaning from text clues.
		Develop writing skills.	Provide basic factual information.	Provide additional detail.	Draw conclusions, express opinions, and do other analysis, synthesis, and evaluation tasks.
Thinking Skills	*What Do You Think?*	Express and support opinions.	Indicate opinions by matching or selecting from multiple-choice items.	React to characters' opinions.	Write sentences expressing and supporting your opinions.
	Culture Clips	Recall key information presented in the *Culture Clips* video segment.	Match art with sentences from the culture clip video segment.	Complete fill-in-the-blank passage on culture clip concepts.	Respond to a situation or express an opinion related to culture clip theme.
	Check Your English	Demonstrate new material mastery.	Match written words with art depicting vocabulary.	Copy words to form a sentence/question using grammatical structure(s) presented in *Your New Language.*	Complete fill-in-the-blank passage that provides a story summary.

The *Photo Stories*

The *Photo Stories* have two primary purposes:

- They serve as a preview activity for viewers with beginning-low (but not literacy-level) English proficiency by assisting them in following the main story line when they view the video. The high-success, low-stress follow-up activities in the Photo Stories are ideal motivators for this group of learners, most of whom could not access the story without this special help.

- They can be used with learners at higher levels to preview and review the story line.

The diagram below and the descriptions that follow illustrate the carefully designed, yet simple and predictable structure of the *Photo Story* episodes.

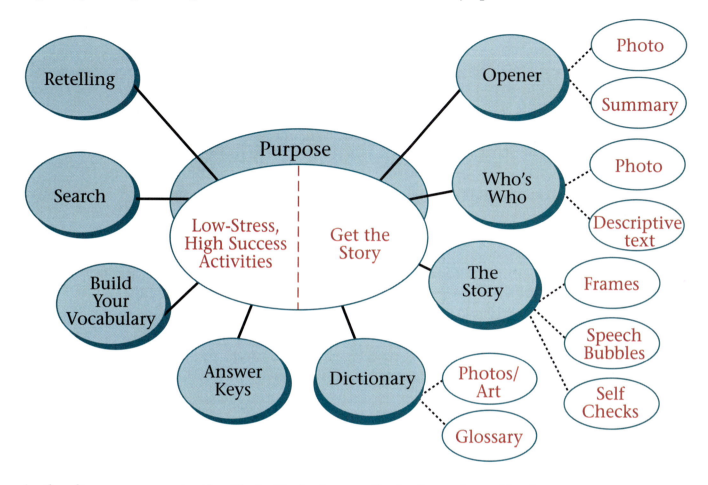

As the diagram suggests, the *Photo Stories* have a limited number of basic components, or elements:

1. **The Unit Opener:** This component helps the learner focus, using a large photo (the same one that appears at the beginning of each *Worktext* unit) that captures the theme of the episode and a capsulized summary statement of only 3 to 5 sentences that provides an overview without giving away the outcome.

2. **Who's Who:** Photos of the characters in the episode that are key to the main story line are included here. Below each photo is the character's name and a phrase describing something about the person that relates to this particular episode. For example, for Katherine in the episode "Family Matters," the phrase reads, "A single mother of two."

3. **The Story:** The story is told with photos from the episode and text, using frames and speech bubbles. Included at appropriate intervals throughout the sequence of frames are comprehension questions with which the student can self-check his or her success at "making meaning." The language "spoken" by the characters in the frames is that heard in the videos, but it is frequently simplified by deleting information, structures, and words.

4. **The Dictionary:** The dictionary provides learners with a resource for clarifying words they do not understand. It has two parts—visuals and glossary. The visuals—photos or art—may be objects, emotions, or actions that can be visually portrayed. The glossary contains six or fewer words that learners encounter in the frames. These words are not easily depicted visually and may require some explanation. The definitions given are very brief and simple. In addition, for each word in the glossary, a sentence other than the one in the video story is provided to model usage.

5. **The Activity Pages:** There are three types of activity pages—Retelling, Searches, and Build Your Vocabulary. In the Retelling activities, learners sequence pictures that represent key elements in the story. The Searches check comprehension of more detailed information, but still focus on the main theme or story line. Answers may be based on text and photo, photo only, or text only. In Build Your Vocabulary, the exercises center around a large picture that shows a scene from the story. The scene selected is rich in vocabulary that is useful to learners but not crucial to the main plot. Items in the picture are numbered, and a vocabulary list keyed to the numbers is provided. Below the pictures and vocabulary list, a series of sentences with blanks in them provides opportunities for learners to put each word into context.

6. **The Answer Keys:** The answers to all activity pages are printed upside down at the bottom of the page on which the exercise falls. The exception is the Check Yourself comprehension questions, whose answers are grouped together on the bottom of the first activity page.

In this way, through a well-designed combination of pictures, text, and language-learning activities, the *Photo Stories* teach basic language and reading-comprehension skills—thus propelling beginning low ESL learners toward higher levels of understanding and fluency.

Teacher's Resource Books

To help classroom teachers and distance-learning instructors give students all the help they need, each of the two *Crossroads Café Teacher's Resource Books* provides general directions for how to work with the program and specific instructions for how to use each episode. Each also has 52 reproducible master activities—4 for each of the 13 episodes in the book—for teachers to copy and give to students to complete in pairs and small groups. By working through these activities, students will be able to engage one another interactively. The following pages are examples of the type of guidance for teachers and activities for students that the *Teacher's Resource Books* provide. With these tools, teachers can make the most effective use of the *Crossroads Café* program during class time.

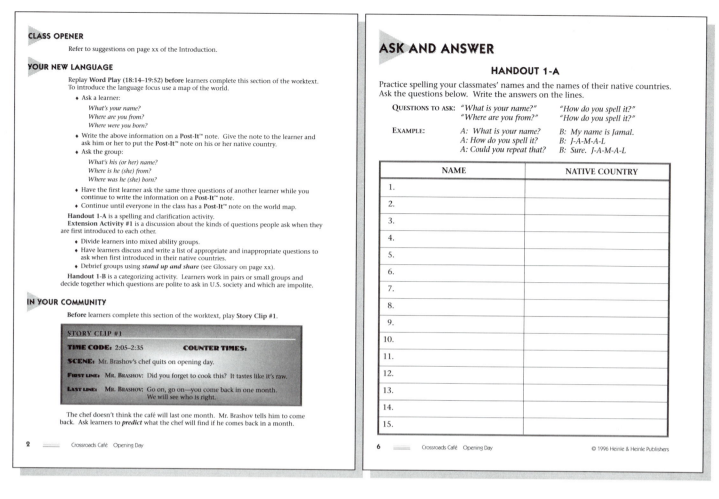

The Crossroads Café Partner's Guide

The *Partner's Guide* is a small book that a formal tutor, a relative, a friend, a coworker, or a neighbor can use to help a learner improve his or her English. This little guide explains, in simple, direct language, what the "helper" can do to make learning with each episode of *Crossroads Café* even better for the learner. The guide provides one page of special instructions for each episode, as well as some general suggestions for a predictable yet lively approach to working with the learner. People who have never taught and seasoned tutors will find a wealth of hints in the *Partner's Guide* for helping learners succeed with their English.

The Crossroads Café Reproducible Master Packet

For the tutor who is working with more than one learner of *Crossroads Café,* the same 104 reproducible masters that are part of the *Teacher's Resource Books* are available separately. The masters can also be used by tutors who want to maximize a single learner's opportunities for interaction by working through the communicative activities in a learning-partner role with the student.

Unit 14: Life Goes On

Before You Watch (page 3)

✪ _3_ medicine   _5_ package
_1_ food tray   _6_ darkness
_4_ nurse   _2_ counter

✪✪ _1_ A young woman gives a package to Jess.
_3_ Mr. Brashov is angry at the nurse.
_5_ Jess explains some things to Rosa and Katherine.
_2_ The patient has something to eat.
_6_ There is a problem with the lights.
_4_ Mr. Brashov takes his medicine.

After You Watch (pages 4 and 5)

✪ 1. c   2. a

✪✪ 1. b   2. e

✪✪✪ 1. a   2. d

✪ 1. no   2. yes   3. no   4. no

✪✪ _2_ While in the hospital, Mr. Brashov meets Joe Jenkins.
_3_ After a few days in the hospital, Mr. Brashov goes home.
_4_ He is happy because he receives a gift from his daughter.
_1_ Mr. Brashov is in the hospital because he had a heart attack.

✪✪✪   Mr. Brashov is in the hospital because he had a heart attack. While in the hospital, Mr. Brashov meets Joe Jenkins. Joe Jenkins likes to talk and joke with the nurse. Mr. Brashov feels sad when Mr. Jenkins dies. After a couple of days in the hospital, Mr. Brashov goes home. When he returns to Crossroads Café, he says he feels glad to be back. He is happy because he receives a gift from his daughter.

Your New Language (pages 6 and 7)

✪ 1. tasteless
2. delicious
3. strict
4. hot

✪✪ 1. b   2. d   3. e   4. a   5. c

✪✪✪ 1. busy   4. work   7. too   10. to work
2. very   5. too   8. to eat   11. very
3. too busy   6. hold   9. too cold

(page 8)

✪ _2_ Mr. Brashov: Why? I am very hungry.
_4_ Mr. Brashov: What can I eat then? The food here is tasteless!
_1_ Brenda: Mr. Brashov, you can't eat that food.
_3_ Brenda: The food is too salty.

✪✪ _3_ Rosa: Then why aren't you eating it?
_2_ Jess: It smells delicious.
_4_ Jess: It's too hot to eat.
_1_ Rosa: How is the chicken and rice?
_5_ Rosa: In a couple of minutes, it will be fine for you to eat.

●●● 5	Jess:	Please let me know when you find the problem.
1	Jess:	When can you fix the fan in the kitchen? It's very hot in there.
4	Jamal:	Don't worry. I'll see what I can do. If it is too expensive to fix, I can buy a new one.
2	Jamal:	I'll go look at it now. It's a very old fan, you know.
3	Jess:	Yes, I know. But I still hope you can fix it. Without a fan in the kitchen, it will be too hot to work.
6	Jamal:	O.K. As soon as I find the problem, I'll figure out how much it's going to cost.

In Your Community (page 9)

✪ 1. aspirin
2. cold, headache, flu, fever, pain
3. 1 or 2 pills
4. upset stomach, dizziness, heartburn

✪✪ 1. No.
2. No.

●●● 1. You should take the medicine with food or milk.
2. You should call your doctor before you take this medicine.

Read and Write (page 10)

Circle the Answers

✪ c   ✪✪ a   ●●● a

Find the Word

✪ a   ✪✪ b   ●●● b

Culture Clip (page 13)

✪ 1. c   2. b   3. a

✪✪ 1. city   5. patients
2. rules   6. short
3. doctors   7. medical care
4. nurses   8. expensive

Check Your English (page 14)

✪ 1. food tray   4. package
2. darkness   5. counter
3. nurses   6. medicine

✪✪ 1. The rules are strict in the hospital. OR Are the rules in the hospital strict?
2. Mr. Brashov is on a very restricted diet. OR Is Mr. Brashov on a very restricted diet?
3. The soup was too hot to eat. OR Was the soup too hot to eat?
4. The meatloaf was too bad to eat. OR Was the meatloaf too bad to eat?

●●● 1. heart attack   5. needs   9. restricted
2. nurse   6. patient   10. complains
3. café   7. dies   11. tasteless
4. organized   8. sad

Unit 15: Breaking Away

Before You Watch (page 17)

✪ _2_ picture   _6_ a family meeting
    _3_ dinner table   _4_ an angry young man
    _5_ an unhappy young woman   _1_ a young couple

✪✪ _6_ Henry is talking with his parents and three other people.
    _5_ The young woman looks unhappy.
    _2_ Edward is looking at a picture.
    _1_ Henry and a young woman are standing very close to each other.
    _4_ Henry looks angry.
    _3_ Henry is sitting at a dinner table with three other people.

After You Watch (page 18)

✪ 1. d   2. d

✪✪ 1. c   2. e

✪✪✪ 1. a   2. b

✪ 1. no   2. yes   3. yes   4. yes

✪✪ _4_ Henry and Sara have a fight.
    _2_ Henry tells his parents that he and Sara are going together.
    _3_ Henry goes to Sara's house for dinner.
    _1_ Henry tells the Crossroads Café employees that he and Sara are going together.
    _5_ Henry asks the parents to come to the café for a meeting.

✪✪✪   Henry tells the Crossroads Café employees that he and Sara are going together. The employees are happy, but not surprised. Henry tells his parents that he and Sara are going together. Mrs. Chang tells Henry that Sara's parents will disapprove of him. Henry goes to Sara's house for dinner. Sara's parents are not happy with the news. Henry and Sara have a fight. Sara tells Henry that he was rude. Henry asks the parents to come to the café for a meeting.

Your New Language (pages 20 and 21)

✪ 1. I like that idea.
    2. I don't like vacant buildings.
    3. I like older women.
    4. I don't like that team.

✪✪ 1. c   2. d   3. e.   4. a   5. b

✪✪✪ 1. don't like   4. don't like
    2. don't like   5. don't like
    3. don't like to   6. like

(page 22)

✪ _2_ I don't like the food there.
    _1_ Let's eat at Mario's tonight.
    _3_ Really! Why not?

✪✪ _3_ That's a dangerous sport.
    _2_ Not really. I like to play hockey.
    _4_ That's true. But it's fun!
    _1_ Do you like to watch football?

✪✪✪ _4_ That doesn't matter. Your customers come here because they like the food.
   _1_ I don't like the laundromat next door.
   _3_ You're right, but it will be noisy. Our customers like to eat in peace and quiet.
   _2_ Why not? At least the building won't be vacant.
   _5_ I know they like the food, but will they like the noise?

In Your Community (page 23)

✪ 1. no   2. yes

✪✪ 1. no   2. no

✪✪✪ 1. no   2. no

Read and Write (page 24)

Circle the Answers

✪ b   ✪✪ a   ✪✪✪ a

Find the Word

✪ 1. going together   2. chance

✪✪ 1. accused   2. disapproval

✪✪✪ 1. proof   2. obvious

Culture Clip (page 27)

✪ 1. c   2. a   3. b

✪✪ 1. couple   4. disagree   7. concerns
   2. adjust   5. decisions   8. appreciation
   3. cultures   6. customs   9. richness

Check Your English (page 28)

✪ 1. dinner table   3. an angry young man   5. a family meeting
   2. a picture   4. an unhappy young woman   6. a young couple

✪✪ 1. I don't like the neigbor next door.
   2. I don't like to watch football.
   3. I really like the food at Crossroads Café.
   4. I like to eat at Chinese restaurants.

✪✪✪ 1. together   6. invites
   2. surprised   7. wait
   3. photograph   8. angry
   4. pleased   9. prejudiced
   5. Chinese   10. meeting

Unit 16: The Bottom Line

Before You Watch (page 31)

✪ _3_ banker   _1_ worried people
   _5_ bingo   _6_ stove part
   _4_ cards   _2_ suit

✪✪ _4_ Some customers play cards, knit, and sleep.
    _6_ Jamal is worried about something.
    _5_ The customers order food and play bingo.
    _2_ Mr. Brashov goes to a bank.
    _1_ Jamal is happy about something.
    _3_ The banker talks to Mr. Brashov about making money.

After You Watch (pages 32 and 33)

✪ 1. d   2. a   3. b

✪✪ 1. f   2. e

✪✪✪ 1. b   2. c

✪ 1. no   2. no   3. no   4. yes

✪✪ _2_ Mr. Brashov needs to borrow money.
    _5_ Mr. Brashov doesn't need money after all.
    _1_ Crossroads Café needs a new oven.
    _4_ Jamal finds the part for the oven.
    _3_ The bank won't loan Mr. Brashov money.

✪✪✪ Crossroads Café needs a new oven. Mr. Brashov needs to borrow money. The bank won't loan Mr. Brashov money. Jess brings friends from the senior citizen center for their morning coffee break. People from the senior center come to eat lunch and play bingo. Mr. Littleton agrees to loan Mr. Brashov money. Jamal finds the part for the oven. Mr. Brashov doesn't need money after all.

Your New Language (pages 34 and 35)

✪ 1. make
   2. attract
   3. give
   4. bring

✪✪ 1. c   2. a   3. d   4. e.   5. b

✪✪✪ 1. told me to   3. said   5. says or said
     2. told me to   4. told me about   6. tell you about

(page 36)

✪ _2_ HENRY: How can he do that?
   _3_ JESS: Well, the bank told him to cut expenses.
   _1_ JESS: The bank told Victor to make more money.

✪✪ _2_ HENRY: Expenses like what?
    _4_ HENRY: So we don't have to worry about our jobs?
    _3_ JAMAL: Mr. Brashov said he could cut food, utilities, or supplies.
    _1_ JAMAL: The bank told Mr. Brashov to reduce expenses.
    _5_ JAMAL: I'm not so sure. Jess said Mr. Brashov could lay off employees.

_3_ ROSA: First of all, Henry told him to go after a younger crowd.

_2_ JESS: Tell me about them.

_8_ JESS: Rosa, how can Victor make money when people buy one and get one free!

_1_ ROSA: We've made several suggestions to Mr. Brashov about how to attract more customers.

_7_ ROSA: He said he's not going to buy high chairs or have little kids spilling milk and breaking glasses. So I told him about a two-for-one special I saw on TV.

_5_ ROSA: Right. Then Katherine told him to make it a family-oriented restaurant.

_4_ JESS: And Victor said they're too noisy. Right?

_6_ JESS: What did Victor think about that?

In Your Community (page 37)

1. $3000
2. He leases. He has a landlord.

1. Yes
2. $9,900 to Larson's Appliances

1. the existing equipment

Read and Write (page 38)

Circle the Answers

b   a   c

Find the Word

c   a   b

Culture Clip (page 41)

1. c   2. d   3. a   4. b

1. roles	4. active	7. help
2. older	5. time	8. library
3. children	6. volunteer	9. grandpas

Check Your English (page 42)

1. bingo game	4. suit
2. cards	5. banker
3. worried people	6. oven part

1. Mr. Littleton told Mr. Brashov to make more money.
2. Rosa told him about a two-for-one special.
3. Mr. Brashov says young people are too noisy.
4. Mr. Brashov said he won't buy day-old bread.

1. working	5. money	9. order
2. parts	6. more	10. game
3. goes	7. wants	11. customers
4. banker	8. citizens	12. loan

Unit 17: United We Stand

Before You Watch (page 45)

✪ 1 faucet   2 pipe
 3 letter   4 check
 5 tenants' meeting   6 signs

✪✪ 5 The tenants are having a meeting about their housing problems.
 2 Jamal is fixing the leaky pipe in Rosa's bathroom.
 6 The tenants have made protest signs.
 1 Rosa is having problems with her faucet.
 3 Rosa is writing a letter of complaint to her building manager.
 4 Rosa is giving her rent check to the building manager.

After You Watch (pages 46 and 47)

✪ 1. b   2. d   3. e

✪✪ 1. a   2. f

✪✪✪ 1. g   2. c

✪ 1. no   2. no   3. yes   4. yes   5. yes

✪✪ 4 The tenants hold a meeting to discuss what to do about the housing problems.
 2 Jamal goes to Rosa's apartment to try to fix Rosa's water problem.
 5 The owner comes to the meeting to hear the complaints.
 1 Rosa has a plumbing problem.
 3 Rosa writes a letter to the building manager describing all the problems.

✪✪✪   Rosa has a plumbing problem. Rosa calls the building manager, but he doesn't answer. Jamal offers to stop by and take a look at Rosa's water problem. Rosa writes a letter to the building manager describing all the problems. The tenants hold a meeting to discuss what to do about the housing problems. A TV reporter comes to the meeting to write a story about the problems. The owner comes to the meeting to hear the complaints. Rosa is invited to talk with the other owners about the problems.

Your New Language (pages 48 and 49)

✪ 1. sink   4. window
 2. stove   5. light switch
 3. air conditioner   6. garbage disposal

✪✪ 1. c   2. e   3. a   4. b   5. d

✪✪✪ 1. rent check   4. water pressure   7. doesn't drain
 2. need some repairs   5. leaks   8. is broken
 3. have problems   6. is peeling   9. When can you

(page 50)

✪ 3 MR. BRASHOV: Did you call your landlord?
 2 ROSA: I'm sorry. I didn't have any water in my apartment this morning. My plumbing doesn't work.
 4 ROSA: Yes, but he wasn't home.
 1 MR. BRASHOV: Rosa, why are you late?

⚫⚫ _4_ ROSA:	Thanks, Jamal. I really appreciate it.	
_1_ JAMAL:	You have a water problem. Not much pressure in the pipes.	
_5_ JAMAL:	You're welcome. But you really should tell your landlord about this soon.	
_2_ ROSA:	Can you fix it?	
_3_ JAMAL:	I'll do my best.	
⚫⚫⚫ _6_ LANDLORD:	O.K. I'll see you at 10:00. O.K.?	
_2_ LANDLORD:	What's the problem?	
_1_ ROSA:	This is Rosa Rivera. Your tenant in apartment C. I have a problem in my apartment.	
_4_ LANDLORD:	Well, I'll need to come and look at the problems first. What's a good day this week?	
_7_ ROSA:	Yes. Thank you.	
_3_ ROSA:	Actually, I have several problems. My faucet leaks in the bathroom, the tile is cracked, the paint is peeling and the sink doesn't drain. When can you fix these things?	
_5_ ROSA:	How about tomorrow? I'm home in the morning.	

In Your Community (page 51)

⚫ 1. 493 Main Street, Apt C, Middletown, IL
  2. $400.00
  3. Robert Ruiz

⚫⚫ 1. 1st of every month, $25.00, 3 days
  2. tenant
  3. yes
  4. to take care of rent that hasn't been paid, to repair damages, to clean

⚫⚫⚫ 1. she can't have a bird, animal, reptile, fish, waterbed or other liquid filled furniture in the apartment

Read and Write (page 52)

Circle the Answers

  ⚫ b   ⚫⚫ b   ⚫⚫⚫ c

Find the Word

  ⚫ 1. d   2. b
  ⚫⚫ 1. c   2. b
  ⚫⚫⚫ 1. a   2. a

Culture Clip (page 55)

  ⚫ 1. d   2. a   3. b   4. c
  ⚫⚫ 1. responsible   2. responsibility   3. tenants   4. owner   5. problem

Check Your English (page 56)

  ⚫ 1. faucet   3. letter   5. tenants' meeting
    2. a pipe   4. check   6. signs

  ⚫⚫ 1. The sink doesn't drain.
    2. The window doesn't open.
    3. The pipe leaks and the tile is cracked.
    4. Is my faucet dripping again? or My faucet is dripping again.

  ⚫⚫⚫ 1. plumbing   5. writes   9. meeting   13. owners
    2. manager   6. elevators   10. reporter
    3. offers   7. dirty   11. problems
    4. water   8. tenants   12. complaints

Unit 18: Opportunity Knocks

Before You Watch (page 59)

✪ _2_ angry person   _3_ cellular phone
   _6_ computer   _1_ jukebox
   _5_ hard hat   _4_ happy people

✪✪ _6_ Jamal works on a computer.
   _2_ Mr. Brashov is angry at Jamal.
   _1_ Two men deliver a jukebox to Crossroads Café.
   _5_ Jamal talks to a man at a construction site.
   _3_ A customer talks on his cellular phone.
   _4_ Jamal and Mr. Brashov are very happy.

After You Watch (pages 60 and 61)

✪ 1. a   2. b

✪✪ 1. d   2. a

✪✪✪ 1. c   2. b

✪ 1. no   2. no   3. yes   4. yes

✪✪ _4_ Jamal quits his engineering job.
   _3_ Jamal becomes unhappy about the materials Mr. Marshall uses in his buildings.
   _1_ One day a customer named Mr. Marshall comes into the café.
   _2_ Jamal leaves Crossroads Café to work as an engineer.

✪✪✪   One day a customer named Mr. Marshall comes into the café. Mr. Marshall owns a construction business and offers Jamal a job. Jamal leaves Crossroads Café to work as an engineer. Jamal becomes unhappy about the materials Mr. Marshall uses in his buildings. He wants Mr. Marshall to stop using old building materials. Mr. Marshall gets angry and wants Jamal to do something wrong. Jamal quits his engineering job. He then goes back to his handyman job at the café.

Your New Language (pages 62 and 63)

✪ 1. nicer   2. busier   3. safer   4. warmer

✪✪ 1. d   2. a   3. b   4. c

✪✪✪ 1. problem   4. building   7. stronger
   2. later   5. newer   8. safety
   3. more   6. old   9. cheaper

(page 64)

✪ _3_ MR. BRASHOV: Good. I hope we stay busy.
   _2_ KATHERINE: Not bad. It was busier than yesterday.
   _4_ KATHERINE: I do, too. I hope we have more customers tomorrow than we did today.
   _1_ MR. BRASHOV: Hello. How was business this morning?

✪✪ _4_ JAMAL: That's not my problem. I am a better engineer than a jukebox repairman.
   _2_ JAMAL: I am not sure. I don't know what is wrong with it.
   _3_ MR. BRASHOV: When you're finished with the toaster can you look at the jukebox?
   _1_ MR. BRASHOV: Can you fix the toaster today?

✪✪✪	_5_ Mr. Brashov:	I don't think so. But I'm not sure. Can you look at these records for me?
	_4_ Henry:	Put in some different records. Rock music is more popular than any other music. Do you have any rock music here?
	_2_ Henry:	I think it's worse than the music we heard yesterday.
	_7_ Mr. Brashov:	That's O.K. You know your music, Henry. I'll try anything you say.
	_3_ Mr. Brashov:	What can I do to make it better?
	_1_ Mr. Brashov:	Henry, how do you like the music in the jukebox today?
	_6_ Henry:	Sure. If we don't have any rock music, you might have to buy some.

In Your Community (page 65)

✪ 1. Regal Engineering and Construction
2. 818 Main Street, Middletown, IL 12345

✪✪ 1. yes   2. no

✪✪✪ 1. No His business does not sell older houses.
2. No Mr. Marshall's company has insurance in case someone gets hurt.
3. No Estimates are free.

Read and Write (page 66)

Circle the Answers

✪ c   ✪✪ c   ✪✪✪ a

Find the Word

✪ b   ✪✪ a   ✪✪✪ a

Culture Clip (page 69)

✪ 1. b   2. c   3. a

✪✪ 1. employers
2. jobs
3. clothing
4. workers
5. worker's compensation
6. expenses
7. unemployment
8. Social Security
9. wives

Check Your English (page 70)

✪ 1. computer
2. hard hat
3. happy people
4. angry person
5. cellular phone
6. jukebox

✪✪ 1. Mr. Brashov wants the café to be busier.
2. Jamal is more worried about safety than Mr. Marshall. OR Is Jamal more worried about safety than Mr. Marshall?
3. Jess is older than Jamal. OR Is Jess older than Jamal?
4. Henry thinks rock music is more popular than polka music.

✪✪✪ 1. music
2. company
3. job
4. computer
5. boss
6. old
7. safe
8. listen
9. money
10. materials
11. engineering
12. handyman

Unit 19: The People's Choice

Before You Watch (page 73)

✪ _2_ election campaign   _4_ speech
   _5_ reporters   _1_ water bill
   _6_ newspaper article   _3_ toupee

✪✪ _4_ Jess is talking to the customers at the café.
   _1_ Mr. Brashov is looking at a water bill.
   _5_ Reporters are listening to Jess' speech.
   _2_ The Crossroads Café employees are putting letters in envelopes.
   _3_ Jess has a toupee on his head.
   _6_ Jess is showing Carol a newspaper article.

After You Watch (pages 74 and 75)

✪ 1. b   2. b

✪✪ 1. d   2. c

✪✪✪ 1. e   2. a

✪ 1. yes   2. yes   3. yes   4. no

✪✪ _5_ Jess loses the election.
   _2_ The Crossroads Café employees want Jess to run for office.
   _1_ Jess is upset because his water bill is incorrect.
   _3_ Dan Miller and Andrew Comstock decide to support Jess.
   _4_ Carol is angry with Jess.

✪✪✪   Jess is upset because his water bill is incorrect. The Crossroads Café employees want Jess to run for office. The employees offer to help him with his campaign. Dan Miller and Andrew Comstock decide to support Jess. They want a candidate who will support business. Carol is angry with Jess. She is unhappy because Jess supports the building of downtown parking structures. Jess loses the election.

Your New Language (pages 76 and 77)

✪ 1. I promise to support the average citizen.
   2. I promise to clean up the city.
   3. I promise to cut taxes.
   4. I promise to stop crime.

✪✪ 1. d   2. e   3. b   4. c   5. a

✪✪✪ 1. promise to work   5. promise to put
   2. promise I will fight   6. promise to repair
   3. promise to establish   7. promised to cut
   4. promise that the garbage will

(page 78)

✪ _2_ JESS: That's what I'm doing.
   _1_ CAROL: You promised to work for the average citizen.
   _3_ CAROL: No, Jess, you're not.

✪✪ _3_ MR. COMSTOCK: I'm sure you will be. I'd like to offer my support. I believe in what you stand for.
   _2_ JESS: Well, I hope they support me. I promise I'll be the best councilman.
   _4_ JESS: Why, thank you. I promise to do a good job.
   _1_ MR. COMSTOCK: Jess, I know a lot of people who are looking for a candiate to support.

✪✪✪ _6_	Jess:	The the same as my interests—safe neighborhoods, a clean city, good schools, and responsive government officials. These are the things I promise to work for.
_2_	Jess:	I promise to work for the average citizen.
_4_	Jess:	It means, I promise I'll listen to your concerns and work for your interests.
_3_	Citizen:	Well that sounds good, but what does it mean?
_1_	Citizen:	What will you do if you are elected to the city council?
_5_	Citizen:	In your opinion, what are my interests?

In Your Community (page 79)

✪ 1. $30,000
  2. 1/9/97

✪✪ 1. 10/13/96 to 12/15/96
   2. call on the telephone or go in person to the office

✪✪✪ 1. look on the reverse side of the bill for information
   2. it's the same

Read and Write (page 80)

Circle the Answers

✪ b   ✪✪ a   ✪✪✪ b

Find the Word

✪ daily   ✪✪ dispute   ✪✪✪ investigate

Culture Clip (page 83)

✪ 1. c   2. a   3. b

✪✪ 1. local   5. govern
   2. executive   6. judicial
   3. official   7. trial
   4. legislative

Check Your English (page 84)

✪ 1. speech   4. reporters
  2. toupee   5. election campaign
  3. water bill   6. newspaper article

✪✪ 1. I promise to help the average citizen.
   2. The city promised to cut taxes.
   3. I promise that I will establish a hot line.
   4. I promise that I will work for you.

✪✪✪ 1. water bill   6. support
    2. incorrect   7. average
    3. run   8. vote
    4. election campaign   9. promises
    5. speeches   10. votes

Unit 20: Outside Looking In

Before You Watch (page 87)

✪ _6_ box   _1_ vase
    _5_ book   _4_ graph
    _3_ painting   _2_ maid

✪✪ _6_ Rosa is arguing with a man.
    _4_ A man is showing people a graph.
    _5_ Rosa is reading a book.
    _2_ A maid is carrying a tray with food.
    _3_ Several people are looking at a painting on the wall.
    _1_ Rosa is looking at a very old vase.

After You Watch (pages 88 and 89)

✪ 1. c.   2. c

✪✪ 1. b   2. a.

✪✪✪ 1. d   2. a

✪ 1. no   2. no   3. yes   4. no

✪✪ _3_ Andrew and Rosa go out on a date.
    _1_ Rosa's teacher, Andrew, comes to the café.
    _4_ Andrew gives Rosa a gift.
    _2_ Rosa goes to a party at Andrew's house.

✪✪✪   Rosa's teacher, Andrew, comes to the café. Andrew asks Rosa for help. Rosa goes to a party at Andrew's house. She translates Spanish into English for the businesspeople. Andrew and Rosa go out on a date. Andrew gives Rosa a gift. Rosa is angry because Andrew is leaving for Europe.

Your New Language (pages 90 and 91)

✪ 1. should try
    2. give me a raise
    3. wear gloves
    4. get more experience

✪✪ 1. d   2. b   3. e   4. a   5. c

✪✪✪ 1. should go   3. should bring
      2. should enroll   4. had better think

(page 92)

✪ _1_ ROSA: You should try our special, Chicken Molé.
   _3_ JESS: Too bad. Rosa's specials are wonderful. You really should try it.
   _2_ ANDREW: Thanks, Rosa, but I'm not hungry.

✪✪ _5_ ROSA: Thanks, Jamal. Those are great ideas.
   _1_ ROSA: I want to talk about art with Andrew.
   _4_ JAMAL: You should also visit some museums.
   _3_ ROSA: That's what I'm planning to do.
   _2_ JAMAL: You should get some books from the library.

✪✪✪	_5_ **KATHERINE:**	I think you should keep busy on the weekends. Let's go to the movies this weekend.
	_3_ **KATHERINE:**	You had better stop that. You know he's not interested in you.
	_2_ **ROSA:**	I don't know. I guess I miss Andrew.
	_1_ **KATHERINE:**	Rosa, what's the matter with you?
	_4_ **ROSA:**	I know that. What do you think I should do?
	_6_ **ROSA:**	Thanks for the advice and the invitation, Katherine.

In Your Community (page 93)

✪ 1. New Park-Park Movie House
2. 11:00, 12:30, 2:30, 4:00, 5:30

✪✪ 1. _Nowhere to be Found, In the Darkness_
2. They are very good movies.

✪✪✪ _Elizabeth's Wedding, Nowhere to be Found_

Read and Write (page 94)

Circle the Answers

✪ b   ✪✪ c   ✪✪✪ a

Find the Word

✪ b   ✪✪ b   ✪✪✪ b

Culture Clip (page 97)

✪ 1. b   2. c   3. a

✪✪ 1. expected   4. worry   7. television
2. raised   5. respect   8. challenging
3. culture   6. goods

Check Your English (page 98)

✪ 1. book   4. maid
2. vase   5. box
3. graph   6. painting

✪✪ 1. You should take him to the movies.
2. You should take a class about modern art.
3. You should bring him by to visit.
4. You had better keep very busy.

✪✪✪ 1. translate   4. impressed   7. dates
2. sophisticated   5. art   8. moving
3. comfortable   6. wines   9. appreciation

Unit 21: Walls and Bridges

Before You Watch (page 101)

✪ _6_ citizenship book   _5_ tailor shop
_1_ lunch box   _3_ skirt
_2_ proud people   _4_ teary eyes

✪✪ _6_ Mr. Brashov studies for the citizenship text.
_3_ A tailor shortens Rosa's skirt.
_1_ A girl hands a man a lunch box.
_5_ Rosa and another woman go to the tailor.
_2_ The girl shows Rosa a photograph.
_4_ The girl is sad.

After You Watch (pages 102 and 103)

✪ 1. b   2. a   3. d

✪✪ 1. d   2. c   3. a

✪✪✪ 1. e   2. d   3. f

✪ 1. yes   2. no   3. yes

✪✪ _3_ Mrs. Scanlon arranges a work-study program for María.
_4_ Mr. Brashov convinces Mr. Hernandez that María should go to school.
_1_ Mrs. Scanlon asks Rosa to talk to María's parents.
_2_ Rosa discovers María is helping out in her father's shop.

✪✪✪   Mrs. Scanlon tells Rosa that María hasn't been going to school. Mrs. Scanlon asks Rosa to talk to María's parents. Rosa discovers María is helping out in her father's shop. María gives Rosa a letter for Mrs. Scanlon. Mrs. Scanlon arranges a work-study program for María. Mrs. Scanlon arranges for a worker in the retraining program to work in Mr. Hernandez's shop. Mr. Brashov convinces Mr. Hernandez that María should go to school.

Your New Language (pages 104 and 105)

✪ 1. Please give her this letter for me.
2. Would you talk to them for me?
3. Would you arrange one for her?
4. I'd be glad to shorten it.

✪✪ 1. e   2. d   3. a   4. c   5. b

✪✪✪ 1. Would you   4. Please help me OR Please
2. Please   5. I'd be glad to
3. I'd be glad to

(page 106)

✪ _2_ KATHERINE: What?
_3_ ROSA: Please explain this word.
_1_ ROSA: Would you do me a favor?

✪✪ _2_ KATHERINE: This box is heavy. Would you help me lift it?
_1_ HENRY: What's wrong?
_4_ KATHERINE: Thanks a lot.
_3_ HENRY: Sure. I'd be glad to lend you a hand.

✪✪✪ _3_ MRS. SCANLON: I don't speak Spanish. Would you translate this note for me?
_5_ MRS. SCANLON: Thanks anyway.
_2_ ROSA: What can I do?
_4_ ROSA: I'm afraid I don't have time right now.
_1_ MRS. SCANLON: I need your help.

In Your Community (page 107)

✪ 1. 6
2. good class participation

✪✪ 1. PE
2. German

✪✪✪ 1. It's probably her favorite subject.
2. She may have gone home in the middle of the day.
3. I would feel good about her grades and about the teachers' comments.

Read and Write (page 108)

Circle the Answers

✪ b   ✪✪ b   ✪✪✪ a

Find the Word

✪ honor student   ✪✪ scholarship   ✪✪✪ big sister program

Culture Clip (page 111)

✪ 1. b   2. c   3. a

✪✪ 1. procedure   4. application   7. government
2. citizenship   5. exam   8. English
3. fingerprints   6. interview   9. citizen

Check Your English (page 112)

✪ 1. citizenship book   4. skirt
2. lunch box   5. teary eyes
3. proud people   6. tailor shop

✪✪ 1. Please help me close this suitcase.
2. Please help María do her homework.
3. I'd be glad to fix that machine for you.
4. Would you define this word for me?

✪✪✪ 1. honor student   5. working
2. college   6. lay off
3. Spanish   7. cry
4. tailor   8. school

Unit 22: Helping Hands

Before You Watch (page 115)

✪ _3_ flashlight   _6_ crib
    _1_ bench   _4_ baby
    _5_ typewriter   _2_ pockets

✪✪ _6_ Jamal is unhappy with Jihan.
     _3_ Jess holds a flashlight for Mr. Brashov.
     _1_ A man sits on a bench outside the café.
     _5_ Henry types something for the man.
     _4_ Jamal enters the hotel room with his baby.
     _2_ The man has his hands in the pockets of his coat.

After You Watch (pages 116 and 117)

✪ 1. a   2. b

✪✪ 1. b   2. c

✪✪✪ 1. a   2. d

✪ 1. no   2. no   3. yes   4. yes

✪✪ _2_ Mr. Brashov helps Frank by giving him some handyman work while Jamal is on vacation.
     _4_ After his second interview, Frank is offered a job as a mechanic.
     _1_ One day, an unemployed man named Frank comes into the café.
     _3_ Frank does excellent work as a handyman, so everybody works together to help him get a new job.

✪✪✪   One day, an unemployed man named Frank comes into the café. He is hungry and asks for something to eat. Everyone thinks that Frank is trying to rob the café, so they put up their hands. After awhile everyone realizes that Frank is not a criminal, but someone who really wants to work. Mr. Brashov helps Frank by giving him some handyman work while Jamal is on vacation. Frank does excellent work as a handyman, so everyone works together to help him get a new job. Frank does not do well in his first job interview, but he gets another chance. After his second interview, Frank is offered a job as a mechanic.

Your New Language (pages 118 and 119)

✪ 1. leave
   2. take
   3. have
   4. go

✪✪ 1. d   2. c   3. a   4. b

✪✪✪ 1. Do you mind   2. May I OR Can I   3. Can I OR May I   4. Do you mind   5. do you mind

(page 120)

✪ _2_ MR. BRASHOV: I guess it's O.K. We're not that busy.
   _1_ KATHERINE: Mr. Brashov, may I leave a little early today?
   _4_ MR. BRASHOV: Why don't you leave now? Call me later to let me know how she is.
   _3_ KATHERINE: Thanks. My daughter is sick and I'm taking her to the doctor.

✪✪ _1_ CUSTOMER: Do you mind if I smoke?
   _4_ KATHERINE: No, no problem. I'll take your drink over for you.
   _2_ KATHERINE: I'm sorry, but smoking is not allowed in this section of the restaurant.
   _3_ CUSTOMER: Do you mind if I move to another table?
   _5_ CUSTOMER: Thanks.

✿✿✿ _4_	JAMAL:	No. This is all I have. Is there something else that could help?
_1_	FRANK:	Can I give you a hand with that pipe?
_6_	JAMAL:	No. I don't mind. I'll use anything that can help me get this pipe back into the sink.
_2_	JAMAL:	Sure. Can you hand me the wrench?
_3_	FRANK:	Sure. Here you go. Don't you have a special wrench for this kind of pipe?
_5_	FRANK:	Yes. Do you mind if we use my wrench instead of this one?

In Your Community (page 121)

✿ 1. 6 months
2. cars, trucks and vans
3. Middletown and Chicago

✿✿ 1. The Neighborhood Service Center.
2. Yes. He operated a tow truck at the Neighborhood Service Center.
3. Yes. He designed a computerized billing system.

✿✿✿ 1. Frank would say that he was a manager of an auto center. He was the supervisor for ten auto mechanics.
2. I don't know. Frank has experience with foreign cars, but it is not indicated on the résumé if he has had any experience repairing air conditioning systems.

Read and Write (page 122)

Circle the Answers

✿ c   ✿✿ b   ✿✿✿ c

Find the Word

✿ c   ✿✿ b   ✿✿✿ b

Culture Clip (page 125)

✿ 1. b   2. d   3. a   4. c

✿✿ 1. earning   5. share
2. money   6. managing
3. families   7. everything
4. children

Check Your English (page 126)

✿ 1. crib   4. flashlight
2. bench   5. baby
3. pockets   6. typewriter

✿✿ 1. May I take your picture for the newspaper?
2. Can I borrow your luggage for my trip?
3. Do you mind if I eat my lunch at noon?
4. Do you mind if I take the kids to the mall?

✿✿✿ 1. unemployed   6. rob   10. job
2. money   7. criminal   11. nervous
3. hungry   8. handyman   12. interview
4. gun   9. vacation   13. mechanic
5. pocket

Unit 23: The Gift

Before You Watch (page 129)

✪ _4_ bills   _3_ mail
     _1_ balloons   _5_ note
     _2_ keys   _6_ birthday party

✪✪ _5_ Jess is reading a note.
     _2_ A man is giving Mr. Brashov a set of keys.
     _4_ Mr. Brashov and a man are going through the bills.
     _6_ Crossroads Café employees are having a birthday party.
     _1_ Henry is holding birthday balloons.
     _3_ Mr. Brashov is looking at the mail.

After You Watch (pages 130 and 131)

✪ 1. c   2. e

✪✪ 1. f   2. b

✪✪✪ 1. d   2. d

✪ 1. yes   2. yes   3. no   4. yes

✪✪ _2_ Joe gives Mr. Brashov the keys to his mountain cabin.
     _1_ Crossroads Café employees plan a surprise birthday party.
     _3_ Emery helps Mr. Brashov with his bills.
     _4_ Mr. Brashov goes to the airport to see his daughter.

✪✪✪   Crossroads Café employees plan a surprise birthday party. The surprise party is for Mr. Brashov. Mr. Brashov invites everyone to dinner as his guests. Joe gives Mr. Brashov the keys to his mountain cabin. The cabin is open this weekend. Emery helps Mr. Brashov with his bills. Mr. Brashov writes Emery a note and leaves the café. Mr. Brashov goes to the airport to see his daughter.

Your New Language (pages 132 and 133)

✪ 1. I'm sorry, but I have a date.
     2. That sounds wonderful, Papa.
     3. I'm afraid I can't. I have too much work.
     4. Thank you, but I have to get back to work.

✪✪ 1. c   2. d   3. a.   4. b

✪✪✪ 1. Would you like   2. Thanks. I'd like to.   3. How about   4. I'm afraid

(page 134)

✪ _3_ MR. BRASHOV: Around 7:00 P.M.
     _2_ JOE: Thanks. That sounds great. What time?
     _1_ MR. BRASHOV: Would you like to come to my birthday party on Saturday?

✪✪ _4_ KATHERINE: I'm sorry. I can't. We're planning to go to the mountains that weekend.
     _1_ ROSA: How about coming over for dinner Friday night?
     _3_ ROSA: Well, how about next weekend?
     _2_ KATHERINE: I'm afraid I can't. I'm going to a concert that night.

✪✪✪	5	**JESS:**	Anna, that's an excuse. Please come.
	3	**JESS:**	Why not? Your dad would be happy to see you.
	6	**ANNA:**	O.K. Jess. I'd really like to. It does sound great!
	1	**JESS:**	We're having a surprise party for your dad. How about coming?
	4	**ANNA:**	Sorry, I'd like to come, but I can't. I don't have a babysitter for Elizabeth.
	2	**ANNA:**	Thanks, Jess. But I'm afraid I can't.

In Your Community (page 135)

✪ 1. Blue Lake Resort
2. boating, fishing, mountain biking, kayaking, horseback riding, lake cruises, water and jet skiing, hiking

✪✪ 1. call for reservations
2. yes; the word *family*

✪✪✪ 1. cabins
2. Route 17 to Carefree Hwy, or Route 17 to Pinnacle Peak Road to Route 60, or Route 17 to Route 60

Read and Write (page 136)

Circle the Answers

✪ c   ✪✪ b   ✪✪✪ c

Find the Word

✪ wonderful   ✪✪ celebrate   ✪✪✪ reason

✪ Happy Birthday! I hope you have a wonderful day. Love,

✪✪ I wish you a happy birthday! Enjoy this very special day. Best wishes,

✪✪✪ Wishing you a very happy birthday on this special day! Best regards,

Culture Clip (page 139)

✪ 1. c   2. b   3. a

✪✪ 1. taxes   4. Property   7. quality
2. income   5. Sales
3. earns   6. benefit

Check Your English (page 140)

✪ 1. mail   4. bills
2. balloons   5. note
3. keys   6. birthday party

✪✪ 1. I'm afraid I can't.
2. Would you like to come with me to the lake this weekend?
3. I'd like to invite you to be my dinner guest.
4. How about going to the movies with me tonight?

✪✪✪ 1. surprise   6. cabin
2. wishes   7. mountains
3. birthday   8. letter
4. invites   9. bills
5. keys   10. balloons

Unit 24: All's Well That Ends Well

Before You Watch (page 143)

✪ _3_ person knocking   _1_ clipboard
    _2_ wedding dress   _6_ people dancing
    _4_ taxicab   _5_ tire

✪✪ _4_ Henry rides in a taxicab.
    _5_ The taxicab has a flat tire.
    _3_ Katherine is very upset.
    _1_ Rosa gives everyone something to do.
    _2_ Bill knocks on the bathroom door.
    _6_ Everyone has a good time at the party.

After You Watch (pages 144 and 145)

✪ 1. f   2. c   3. g

✪✪ 1. e   2. b   3. c

✪✪✪ 1. d   2. a   3. h

✪ 1. no   2. yes   3. no   4. no

✪✪ _2_ However, there are many problems.
    _3_ Katherine gets upset about all the problems and locks herself in the bathroom.
    _1_ The workers are very busy getting the café ready for a party.
    _4_ After a while, Katherine comes out of the bathroom and everyone has a good time at the party.

✪✪✪   The workers are very busy getting the café ready for a party. The party is for Bill and Katherine, who are getting married. However, there are many problems. The airport may close because of a snowstorm. Also, the photographer is sick and cannot take the wedding pictures. Katherine gets upset about all the problems and locks herself in the bathroom. While she is in the bathroom, many people come to the café for the party. After a while, Katherine comes out of the bathroom and everyone has a good time at the party.

Your New Language (pages 146 and 147)

✪ 1. be   2. pick up   3. take   4. be late

✪✪ 1. b   2. c   3. a   4. d

✪✪✪ 1. going   5. am going   8. will   11. will
    2. am going   6. are going   9. going to   12. will
    3. will   7. are going   10. will   13. is going
    4. going to

(page 148)

✪ _3_ Rosa: Sure, I'll help you.
    _1_ Rosa: We have a lot to do to get ready for this dinner. So what are we going to do first?
    _2_ Jamal: We'll need to clean off all the tables. Then we'll have to move them around. Will you be able to help me out?
    _4_ Jamal: After we finish with the tables, I am going to set up all the chairs.

✪✪ _4_ Calli: Don't worry. You'll be safe with me. I take care of all my passengers.
    _5_ Henry: That's good news. Now I'll be able to relax a little and enjoy the trip.
    _2_ Calli: No problem. But there's a lot of snow out there. It's going to take a long time to get there.
    _1_ Henry: I'm going to meet someone at the airport. Will you be able to get there O.K.?
    _3_ Henry: That's O.K. I don't care how long it takes. I just hope we'll get there safely.

4 KATHERINE: I don't care. I'll come out when I feel better. But right now, I am going to stay right here.

3 BILL: You have to. Darling, everybody is going to be here soon and they will want to meet you.

2 KATHERINE: No, it isn't. My dress is going to look terrible. We won't have any wedding pictures because the photographer won't be here. All the snow . . . why should I come out?

6 KATHERINE: Then they will have to use the bathroom next door!

5 BILL: But you can't stay in there all night. You are going to have to come out sometime. When everybody gets here, someone will need to use the bathroom.

1 BILL: Honey, will you please come out of the bathroom? Everything is going to be all right.

In Your Community (page 149)

✪ 1. Jess and Carol Washington
   2. Friday, November 10th
   3. at Crossroads Café

✪✪ 1. For four hours; from 7 to 11.
   2. Victor Brashov and Rosa are giving the party.
   3. No, it's a dinner party.

✪✪✪ 1. You should call either Victor Brashov or Rosa Rivera and tell them whether you can go.
   2. No, because the invitation says formal dress.

Read and Write (page 150)

Circle the Answers

✪ c   ✪✪ c   ✪✪✪ b

Find the Word

✪ b   ✪✪ b   ✪✪✪ a

Culture Clip (page 153)

✪ 1. c   2. b   3. a

✪✪ 1. marriage   4. clothes   7. groom
   2. customs   5. family   8. toasts
   3. wedding   6. gifts   9. ceremony

Check Your English (page 154)

✪ 1. dancing people   3. taxicab   5. clipboard
   2. tire   4. person knocking 6. wedding dress

✪✪ 1. We are going to have a lot of snow. OR Are we going to have a lot of snow?
   2. Lars will arrive at the party late. OR Will Lars arrive at the party late?
   3. Bill and Katherine are going to get married tomorrow. OR Are Bill and Katherine going to get married tomorrow?
   4. Mr. Brashov will make a toast to Bill and Katherine. OR Will Mr. Brashov make a toast to Bill and Katherine?

✪✪✪ 1. married   5. grandfather   9. wedding dress   13. family
   2. problems   6. sad   10. bathroom
   3. snowstorm   7. photographer   11. arrive
   4. airport   8. wedding   12. happy

Unit 25: Comings and Goings

Before You Watch (page 157)

✪ _2_ dinner guest   _4_ cash register
 _5_ gift   _1_ CD (compact disc)
 _3_ singer   _6_ sad people

✪✪ _4_ Katherine teaches a woman to use the cash register.
 _5_ Katherine and Suzanne open a gift.
 _1_ The man listens to a lot of CDs in his office.
 _6_ The guests at the party become sad.
 _3_ Henry's band plays at Crossroads Café.
 _2_ Jamal and Jihan have dinner with a friend.

After You Watch (pages 158 and 159)

✪ 1. f   2. c   3. h

✪✪ 1. d   2. f   3. a

✪✪✪ 1. g   2. b   3. e

✪ 1. yes   2. no   3. no   4. no

✪✪ _2_ Katherine quits her job and helps find a new waitress.
 _4_ Everyone at the party becomes sad when Mr. Brashov gets a phone call from Carol Washington.
 _3_ The café workers have a going-away party for Katherine.
 _1_ The workers at Crossroads Café make changes in their lives.

✪✪✪   The workers at Crossroads Café make changes in their lives. Katherine quits her job and helps find a new waitress. Besides Katherine, Henry and Jamal also are given chances to make changes in their jobs. Henry and his band play their music for a record producer. Jamal is offered an engineering job. The café workers have a going-away party for Katherine. Everyone at the party becomes sad when Mr. Brashov gets a phone call from Carol Washington. Carol tells Mr. Brashov that Jess was in a car accident and he died.

Your New Language (pages 160 and 161)

✪ 1. play   2. ask   3. arrive   4. win

✪✪ 1. b.   2. d   3. c   4. a

✪✪✪ 1. going to go   3. am going to   5. might   7. might
 2. am going to   4. are going to   6. am going to

(page 162)

✪ _3_ JAMAL: What else do you think you might do?
 _2_ KATHERINE: First of all, I will spend more time with my kids.
 _1_ JAMAL: What are you going to do?
 _4_ KATHERINE: I might go to school.

✪✪ _3_ HENRY: Yes, but you will really like our music.
 _6_ DANNY: Yes. Give me a call tomorrow. I am going to be out of the office in the morning, but I should be back around two o'clock.
 _2_ DANNY: I might. You know I listen to a lot of bands just like you.
 _4_ DANNY: Maybe that's true, but I have a business meeting in about fifteen minutes. I might have some time later this afternoon to listen to it.
 _1_ HENRY: Are you going to listen to our tape?
 _5_ HENRY: Oh. So, should we call you?

○○○ _4_ MR. BRASHOV:	I don't know, but I am going to miss her. We're all a big family here.
_1_ JESS:	What's the matter, Victor? You look worried.
_2_ MR. BRASHOV:	Well, for one thing, Katherine is leaving us. She says she's going to spend more time with her kids, and she might go to law school.
_3_ JESS:	That's wonderful. But what are you going to do without Katherine?
_6_ MR. BRASHOV:	I hope you are going to keep coming in even after Katherine leaves. I might get bored if I don't get the chance to beat you in chess.
_5_ JESS:	That's the truth. That's why I enjoy coming here so much.
_7_ JESS:	Don't worry, my friend. I'll be drinking coffee here for a long, long time.

In Your Community (page 163)

✪ 1. full-time   2. yes   3. S

✪✪ 1. The application says the questions marked by an * are optional. She doesn't have to answer questions 3, 5, and 12, and the questions about age, sex, and race/ethnicity.
2. No, because she graduated from high school.
3. Yes, a check for $30.00.

✪✪✪ 1. No, all applications for the fall semester had to be received by February 1. Her application is dated 2/16.
2. No, because Katherine's family makes $32,500, which is more than $23,200.

Read and Write (page 164)

Circle the Answers

✪ b   ✪✪ b   ✪✪✪ a

Find the Word

✪ b   ✪✪ a   ✪✪✪ c

Culture Clip (page 167)

✪ 1. b   2. c   3. a

✪✪ 1. return	4. war	7. strange
2. native	5. desire	8. belong
3. visit	6. ways	9. comfortable

Check Your English (page 168)

✪ 1. gift	4. sad people
2. singer	5. cash register
3. dinner guest	6. CDs or compact discs

✪✪ 1. Henry is going to get a record contract. OR Is Henry going to get a record contract?
2. Jamal and Jihan are going to move back to Egypt. OR Are Jamal and Jihan going to move back to Egypt?
3. Jess might win the big chess game. OR Might Jess win the big chess game?
4. Katherine might become a lawyer. OR Might Katherine become a lawyer?

✪✪✪ 1. workers	6. record	10. decide
2. changes	7. contract	11. party
3. waitress	8. Egypt	12. happy
4. school	9. discuss	13. died
5. band		

Unit 26: Winds of Change

Before You Watch (page 171)

✪ _6_ happy people   _4_ envelope
    _3_ college catalogue   _2_ chess board
    _1_ carton   _5_ bandage

✪✪ _4_ Carol gives Mr. Brashov an envelope.
    _1_ Jamal packs his tools in a shipping carton.
    _6_ Rosa and Mr. Brashov are happy.
    _5_ Marie puts a bandage on Henry's hand.
    _2_ Mr. Brashov gives the chess board to Carol.
    _3_ Rosa and Henry look at Katherine's college catalogue.

After You Watch (pages 172 and 173)

✪ 1. e   2. d   3. b

✪✪ 1. h   2. c   3. g

✪✪✪ 1. a   2. f   3. b

✪ 1. no   2. yes   3. no   4. no

✪✪ _3_ Mr. Brashov thinks about selling the café.
    _4_ In addition to Jamal, Jihan, and Mr. Brashov, Henry makes a decision that will change his life.
    _1_ The Crossroads Café workers make decisions about the future.
    _2_ For example, Jamal and Jihan decide about Jamal's job offer in Egypt.

✪✪✪   The Crossroads Café workers make decisions about the future. For example, Jamal and Jihan decide about Jamal's job offer in Egypt. They finally decide that Egypt is their home and they can have a good life there. Mr. Brashov thinks about selling the café. He finally decides not to sell and asks Rosa to be the new manager. In addition to Jamal, Jihan, and Mr. Brashov, Henry makes a decision that will change his life. Although Henry still loves his music, he decides to go to college to expand his opportunities for the future.

Your New Language (pages 174 and 175)

✪ 1. stay   2. buy   3. keep   4. take

✪✪ 1. c   2. d   3. a   4. b

✪✪✪ 1. come   3. keep   5. try   7. be
     2. have   4. must   6. must

(page 176)

✪ _3_ JIHAN: Why? Is there a problem at the café?
    _2_ JAMAL: Oh, I have to work late tomorrow night.
    _1_ JIHAN: What's the matter, Jamal?
    _4_ JAMAL: Yes. I have to replace some parts in the heating system.

✪✪ _3_ HENRY: I know, but I had to do the dishes in a hurry. One of the glasses broke in the sink. I can't stop the bleeding.
    _5_ HENRY: Thank you. Is there anything more I have to do?
    _2_ MARIE: You must be more careful.
    _1_ HENRY: Oh great! I cut my hand!
    _6_ MARIE: No, not really. But you must keep it clean and dry.
    _4_ MARIE: You can't? Let me take a look. I don't think you will have to get stitches. I'll just put a bandage on it for now.

_4_ KATHERINE:	I have to take a math class and a writing class. I can choose the others.
_7_ ROSA:	Why? Can't Bill watch the kids at night?
_2_ KATHERINE:	Oh, it's the catalogue from City College. I have to choose some classes.
_6_ KATHERINE:	No, I must go to school during the day when my kids are at school.
_1_ ROSA:	What are you reading?
_8_ KATHERINE:	Sometimes Bill has to work at night. And I really can't afford a babysitter very often.
_3_ ROSA:	What classes are you thinking about?
_5_ ROSA:	Are they night classes?

In Your Community (page 177)

✪ 1. 9 buildings   2. The library   3. In Building F   4. Building C (Computer science)

✪✪ 1. Bus stop Y
2. No. There are no building entrances on Carlsburg Boulevard.

✪✪✪ 1. It is the only building that has two separate entrances. OR It is in the middle of the campus.
2. You have to walk south on Eugene Avenue until you get to 14th Street. You then turn left onto 14th Street and walk straight until you get to the corner of Carlsburg Boulevard and 14th Street. You then enter the library on 14th Street.

Read and Write (page 178)

Circle the Answers

✪ b   ✪✪ c   ✪✪✪ c

Find the Word

✪ b   ✪✪ a   ✪✪✪ c

Culture Clip (page 181)

✪ 1. b   2. c   3. a

✪✪
1. graduation	4. employee	7. goals
2. English	5. degrees	8. meaning
3. student	6. radio	9. children

Check Your English (page 182)

✪
1. carton	4. bandage
2. chess board	5. envelope
3. college catalogue	6. happy people

✪✪ 1. He has to take his sick baby to the doctor.
2. Henry must make a decision about school.
3. My brother has to ride a bus to work every day.
4. A student must study hard to get good grades.

✪✪✪
1. good-bye	5. accepts	9. college
2. spend	6. decide	10. told
3. manager	7. study	11. wait
4. decision	8. lawyer	12. time

Student Checklist

UNIT 14

Level	★	★★	★★★
Before You Watch	____ out of 6	____ out of 6	____ out of 6
After You Watch	____ out of 2	____ out of 2	____ out of 2
	____ out of 4	____ out of 4	____ out of 7
Your New Language	____ out of 4	____ out of 5	____ out of 11
	____ out of 4	____ out of 5	____ out of 6
In Your Community	____ out of 4	____ out of 2	____ out of 2
Read and Write	____ out of 1	____ out of 1	____ out of 1
	____ out of 1	____ out of 1	____ out of 1
Culture Clip	____ out of 3	____ out of 8	_____
Check Your English	____ out of 6	____ out of 4	____ out of 11
TOTAL	____ **out of 35**	____ **out of 38**	____ **out of 47**

UNIT 15

Level	★	★★	★★★
Before You Watch	____ out of 6	____ out of 6	____ out of 6
After You Watch	____ out of 2	____ out of 2	____ out of 2
	____ out of 4	____ out of 5	____ out of 9
Your New Language	____ out of 4	____ out of 5	____ out of 6
	____ out of 3	____ out of 4	____ out of 5
In Your Community	____ out of 2	____ out of 2	____ out of 2
Read and Write	____ out of 1	____ out of 1	____ out of 1
	____ out of 2	____ out of 2	____ out of 2
Culture Clip	____ out of 3	____ out of 9	_____
Check Your English	____ out of 6	____ out of 4	____ out of 10
TOTAL	____ **out of 33**	____ **out of 40**	____ **out of 43**

UNIT 16

Level	⭐	⭐⭐	⭐⭐⭐
Before You Watch	_____ out of 6	_____ out of 6	_____ out of 6
After You Watch	_____ out of 3	_____ out of 2	_____ out of 2
	_____ out of 4	_____ out of 5	_____ out of 8
Your New Language	_____ out of 4	_____ out of 5	_____ out of 6
	_____ out of 3	_____ out of 5	_____ out of 8
In Your Community	_____ out of 2	_____ out of 2	_____ out of 1
Read and Write	_____ out of 1	_____ out of 1	_____ out of 1
	_____ out of 1	_____ out of 1	_____ out of 1
Culture Clip	_____ out of 4	_____ out of 9	_____
Check Your English	_____ out of 6	_____ out of 4	_____ out of 12
TOTAL	**_____ out of 34**	**_____ out of 40**	**_____ out of 45**

UNIT 17

Level	⭐	⭐⭐	⭐⭐⭐
Before You Watch	_____ out of 6	_____ out of 6	_____ out of 6
After You Watch	_____ out of 3	_____ out of 2	_____ out of 2
	_____ out of 5	_____ out of 5	_____ out of 10
Your New Language	_____ out of 6	_____ out of 5	_____ out of 9
	_____ out of 4	_____ out of 5	_____ out of 7
In Your Community	_____ out of 3	_____ out of 4	_____ out of 2
Read and Write	_____ out of 1	_____ out of 1	_____ out of 1
	_____ out of 2	_____ out of 2	_____ out of 2
Culture Clip	_____ out of 4	_____ out of 5	_____
Check Your English	_____ out of 6	_____ out of 4	_____ out of 13
TOTAL	**_____ out of 40**	**_____ out of 39**	**_____ out of 52**

Unit 18

Level	⭐	✪✪	✪✪✪
Before You Watch	___ out of 6	___ out of 6	___ out of 6
After You Watch	___ out of 2	___ out of 2	___ out of 2
	___ out of 4	___ out of 4	___ out of 8
Your New Language	___ out of 4	___ out of 4	___ out of 9
	___ out of 4	___ out of 4	___ out of 7
In Your Community	___ out of 2	___ out of 2	___ out of 3
Read and Write	___ out of 1	___ out of 1	___ out of 1
	___ out of 1	___ out of 1	___ out of 1
Culture Clip	___ out of 3	___ out of 9	_____
Check Your English	___ out of 6	___ out of 4	___ out of 12
TOTAL	___ **out of 33**	___ **out of 37**	___ **out of 49**

Unit 19

Level	⭐	✪✪	✪✪✪
Before You Watch	___ out of 6	___ out of 6	___ out of 6
After You Watch	___ out of 2	___ out of 2	___ out of 2
	___ out of 4	___ out of 5	___ out of 8
Your New Language	___ out of 4	___ out of 5	___ out of 7
	___ out of 3	___ out of 4	___ out of 6
In Your Community	___ out of 2	___ out of 2	___ out of 2
Read and Write	___ out of 1	___ out of 1	___ out of 1
	___ out of 1	___ out of 1	___ out of 1
Culture Clip	___ out of 3	___ out of 7	_____
Check Your English	___ out of 6	___ out of 4	___ out of 10
TOTAL	___ **out of 32**	___ **out of 37**	___ **out of 43**

UNIT 20

Level	⭐	⭐⭐	⭐⭐⭐
Before You Watch	____ out of 6	____ out of 6	____ out of 6
After You Watch	____ out of 2	____ out of 2	____ out of 2
	____ out of 4	____ out of 4	____ out of 7
Your New Language	____ out of 4	____ out of 5	____ out of 4
	____ out of 3	____ out of 5	____ out of 6
In Your Community	____ out of 2	____ out of 2	____ out of 2
Read and Write	____ out of 1	____ out of 1	____ out of 1
	____ out of 1	____ out of 1	____ out of 1
Culture Clip	____ out of 3	____ out of 8	_____
Check Your English	____ out of 6	____ out of 4	____ out of 9
TOTAL	____ **out of 32**	____ **out of 38**	____ **out of 38**

UNIT 21

Level	⭐	⭐⭐	⭐⭐⭐
Before You Watch	____ out of 6	____ out of 6	____ out of 6
After You Watch	____ out of 3	____ out of 3	____ out of 3
	____ out of 3	____ out of 4	____ out of 7
Your New Language	____ out of 4	____ out of 5	____ out of 5
	____ out of 3	____ out of 4	____ out of 5
In Your Community	____ out of 2	____ out of 2	____ out of 3
Read and Write	____ out of 1	____ out of 1	____ out of 1
	____ out of 1	____ out of 1	____ out of 1
Culture Clip	____ out of 3	____ out of 9	_____
Check Your English	____ out of 6	____ out of 4	____ out of 8
TOTAL	____ **out of 32**	____ **out of 39**	____ **out of 39**

UNIT 22

Level	★	★★	★★★
Before You Watch	____ out of 6	____ out of 6	____ out of 6
After You Watch	____ out of 2	____ out of 2	____ out of 2
	____ out of 4	____ out of 4	____ out of 8
Your New Language	____ out of 4	____ out of 4	____ out of 5
	____ out of 4	____ out of 5	____ out of 6
In Your Community	____ out of 3	____ out of 3	____ out of 2
Read and Write	____ out of 1	____ out of 1	____ out of 1
	____ out of 1	____ out of 1	____ out of 1
Culture Clip	____ out of 4	____ out of 7	_____
Check Your English	____ out of 6	____ out of 4	____ out of 13
TOTAL	____ **out of 36**	____ **out of 37**	____ **out of 44**

UNIT 23

Level	★	★★	★★★
Before You Watch	____ out of 6	____ out of 6	____ out of 6
After You Watch	____ out of 2	____ out of 2	____ out of 2
	____ out of 4	____ out of 4	____ out of 8
Your New Language	____ out of 4	____ out of 4	____ out of 4
	____ out of 3	____ out of 4	____ out of 6
In Your Community	____ out of 2	____ out of 2	____ out of 2
Read and Write	____ out of 1	____ out of 1	____ out of 1
	____ out of 1	____ out of 1	____ out of 1
Culture Clip	____ out of 3	____ out of 7	_____
Check Your English	____ out of 6	____ out of 4	____ out of 10
TOTAL	____ **out of 32**	____ **out of 35**	____ **out of 40**

UNIT 24

Level	★	★★	★★★
Before You Watch	____ out of 6	____ out of 6	____ out of 6
After You Watch	____ out of 3	____ out of 3	____ out of 3
	____ out of 4	____ out of 4	____ out of 8
Your New Language	____ out of 4	____ out of 4	____ out of 13
	____ out of 4	____ out of 5	____ out of 6
In Your Community	____ out of 3	____ out of 3	____ out of 2
Read and Write	____ out of 1	____ out of 1	____ out of 1
	____ out of 1	____ out of 1	____ out of 1
Culture Clip	____ out of 3	____ out of 9	_____
Check Your English	____ out of 6	____ out of 4	____ out of 13
TOTAL	____ **out of 35**	____ **out of 40**	____ **out of 53**

UNIT 25

Level	★	★★	★★★
Before You Watch	____ out of 6	____ out of 6	____ out of 6
After You Watch	____ out of 3	____ out of 3	____ out of 3
	____ out of 4	____ out of 4	____ out of 8
Your New Language	____ out of 4	____ out of 4	____ out of 7
	____ out of 4	____ out of 6	____ out of 7
In Your Community	____ out of 3	____ out of 3	____ out of 2
Read and Write	____ out of 1	____ out of 1	____ out of 1
	____ out of 1	____ out of 1	____ out of 1
Culture Clip	____ out of 4	____ out of 9	_____
Check Your English	____ out of 6	____ out of 4	____ out of 13
TOTAL	____ **out of 35**	____ **out of 38**	____ **out of 39**

UNIT 26

Level	⭐	⭐⭐	⭐⭐⭐
Before You Watch	____ out of 6	____ out of 6	____ out of 6
After You Watch	____ out of 3	____ out of 3	____ out of 3
	____ out of 4	____ out of 4	____ out of 8
Your New Language	____ out of 4	____ out of 4	____ out of 7
	____ out of 4	____ out of 6	____ out of 8
In Your Community	____ out of 4	____ out of 2	____ out of 2
Read and Write	____ out of 1	____ out of 1	____ out of 1
	____ out of 1	____ out of 1	____ out of 1
Culture Clip	____ out of 3	____ out of 9	_____
Check Your English	____ out of 6	____ out of 4	____ out of 12
TOTAL	____ **out of 36**	____ **out of 40**	____ **out of 48**

Index